MW01717564

An Adventurous Journey

Richard W. Hale

Printed in the United States of America

Book-broker Publishers of Florida
Port Charlotte, FL 33980
ISBN 978-1-945690-62-4

This book is dedicated to my family,
with special thanks and mention to
Diane, my wife,
for her constant dedication,
sensitivity, and encouragement.

TABLE OF CONTENTS

PROLOGUE

Over the years as I have related my stories and experiences verbally during general conversations with friends and family, some of them have said, "Dick you should write a book about all of your adventures."

I am one who has never thought my experiences were unique or interesting enough to warrant a book, so I have always resisted those requests - until now.

This book then, is a retelling of a few of those experiences and adventures. Within the narrative, I have sought to include an overall theme about the power of a very basic human emotion – "rejection." The power I speak of can manifest itself in several different forms: antipathy, anger, sorrow, to name just a few.

This story chronicles the impact of anger. That anger was the underlying source of drive for me to always prove that I wasn't a "throwaway," that I was just as good as anybody else.

Anger can be a force for good, and it can also be a cause of bad things happening. This book contains both.

It is my hope that some of these real-life events can serve as a guide to be on the lookout for "the slings and arrows of outrageous fortune," as Shakespeare said. This story is also about the importance of family and heritage.

I hope you enjoy the tale!

RAGE

It was cold, and snow was starting to fall. The field was six inches of mud, and my blue and gold uniform was now totally brown. You couldn't even see the numbers. Football in Michigan in the late fall, you've got to love it. In the fourth quarter with a little over three minutes to go, we were leading thirteen to seven. But if they scored and kicked the extra point we would lose. They had been gaining every play off the left side and were now down to our ten-yard line.

The coach called time-out. We went over to the bench to see if we could regroup.

"Hale, switch over to the left end position, they're running that sweep and if you can get some penetration, I think we can stop them." Coach Kjolhede told me. "Donnell, from your halfback position, if you see that Hale has turned them in, go right in after him and make the tackle. Don't worry about a pass, they're not going to throw the ball. Come on, girls!"

We ran back on to the field. I walked, because something was happening to me, something I knew well. I was getting really, really, angry. If they scored, our undefeated season, my senior year season, and a shot at the class A High School State Championship, which Battle Creek had never won, would all go down the tubes. Bullshit! I was 6-foot-three and 200 pounds, they were going to have to go through me and that was not going to happen! I was really angry.

They ran four straight plays at me and I went crazy, throwing guys off me left and right. I made the tackle on three of the four plays and Donnell finished them off on the fourth. I was screaming and yelling at my teammates about getting some guts and not giving up. Nobody even looked at me, they were scared.

We stopped them on the ten, won the game, remained undefeated, and won Battle Creek Central's first Michigan Class A Championship. As we were walking off the field to the locker-room for a shower, Coach Kjolhede came up to me

"That's the way to play defense, Hale, good job."

Ted Kjolhede was one tough son of a bitch, but he, with those simple words, made my day!

Nobody else talked to me just then, I think I scared them. Shit, I scared myself. People kept looking at me, then away. What the hell happened? I had lost control. My anger had a focal point and I had made the most of it. It just happened, and I didn't control it. That anger made me good at football, basketball, and getting in fights. Two out of three isn't bad-right?

Where did this anger come from? And why was it always there in my life, hiding out and waiting for an opportunity to roar full-bore at whatever stood in my way? What was I trying to prove?

CONFUSION

When I was eight years old, I stumbled onto a document that said to me that my whole life was a lie. The papers indicated that my name was not Richard William Hale, and that my parents were not Robert and Donna Hale. The paper indicated that my name had been changed and that I had been adopted February 17, 1942, when I was five years old. I had been given to my foster parents at age two, then formally adopted when I was five years old. My name had been changed from Gayle Eugene Llewelyn, my birth name, to Richard William Hale. The sudden realization that my parents weren't my parents was a shock. What happened to my family? Who were they? Who was I?

That memory may have faded along with skinned knees and bruised elbows, but what made it real and powerful was my mother's reaction.

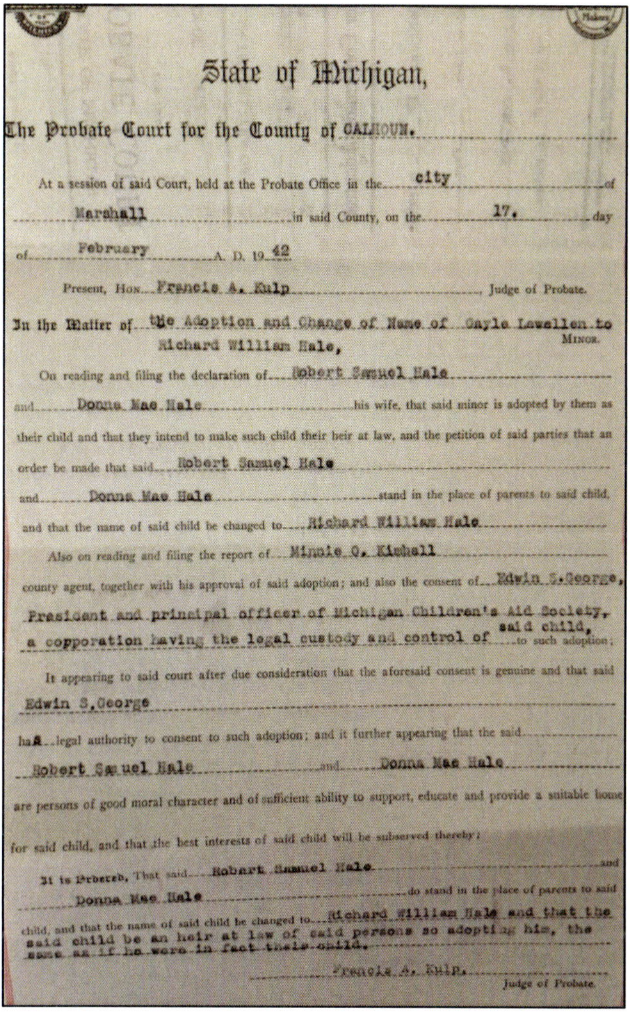

State of Michigan,

The Probate Court for the County of CALHOUN.

At a session of said Court, held at the Probate Office in the city of Marshall in said County, on the 17. day of February A. D. 1942

Present, Hon. Francis A. Kulp, Judge of Probate.

In the Matter of the Adoption and Change of Name of Gayle Lewellen to Richard William Hale, Minor.

On reading and filing the declaration of Robert Samuel Hale and Donna Mae Hale his wife, that said minor is adopted by them as their child and that they intend to make such child their heir at law, and the petition of said parties that an order be made that said Robert Samuel Hale and Donna Mae Hale stand in the place of parents to said child, and that the name of said child be changed to Richard William Hale.

Also on reading and filing the report of Minnie O. Kimball county agent, together with his approval of said adoption; and also the consent of Edwin S. George, President and principal officer of Michigan Children's Aid Society, a copporation having the legal custody and control of said child, to such adoption;

It appearing to said court after due consideration that the aforesaid consent is genuine and that said Edwin S. George has legal authority to consent to such adoption; and it further appearing that the said Robert Samuel Hale and Donna Mae Hale are persons of good moral character and of sufficient ability to support, educate and provide a suitable home for said child, and that the best interests of said child will be subserved thereby;

It is Ordered, That said Robert Samuel Hale and Donna Mae Hale do stand in the place of parents to said child, and that the name of said child be changed to Richard William Hale and that the said child be an heir at law of said persons so adopting him, the same as if he were in fact their child.

Francis A. Kulp,
Judge of Probate.

The document that started it all

Robert Samuel, Donna May, and newly named Richard William Hale - age 5.

"Don't ever bring this up again," she shouted, her face flushed with anger. She snatched the document away from me. "Forget it, it has nothing to do with you."

I never brought it up again, but I never forgot it either! I found out much later that my birth mother was unmarried and she felt that she could not care for me adequately either financially or emotionally so she gave me up for adoption and I became a ward of the Children's Aid Society of Michigan.

My memories of that time period are foggy at best with some memory of having to get all dressed up and traveling in the car with my adoptive parents to a meeting with a nice lady who looked me over and asked me a bunch of questions. This happened several times. I can only surmise that this was a representative of the Children's Aid Society who was making sure that I was not being abused. These visits clearly happened before the adoption date.

My new father was a schoolteacher and the director of industrial training for the school system and my new mother was a part time secretary and homemaker.

We lived in Battle Creek, Michigan in a two-bedroom home where I had a bedroom all to myself – until my newly adopted sister showed up. Then I had to move into the basement where I slept on a couch.

My earliest memory of my sister is of riding home in the car from someplace, probably Lansing, where the Children's Aid Society was located. I was asked what I thought her name should be. She was little then, sitting in the back seat with me, and

Marj and me. I was in eighth grade, she was four years behind me.

quiet as a mouse. As I recall, that was probably the only time she was quiet.

As we grew up, my younger sister was a veritable pain in the ass because she was always following me around. I was her big brother and she always wanted to be involved in whatever I was doing.

She was four years behind me in school so we were never in the same school, something I was always thankful for, but we did grow up together.

She was named Marjorie Jean Hale—should have been "Miss Goody Two-Shoes." I mean, if I did everything wrong, she did everything right. I was constantly in trouble, primarily with my mother who was German, very proud, very tough and stubborn, unfortunately, just like me. We were a family, with the normal family dynamics.

When I graduated from high school, I went into the Navy. When my sister graduated four years later, she went to college where she met her future husband.

We were, and are today, brother and sister. We have shared our lives together, love each other, and always will. We are brother and sister, better than most.

* * *

My father had quite a life. He grew up in Escanaba Michigan in the Upper Peninsula of Northern Michigan. It turns out that when he was in his senior class, while in high school, he was taking a course in auto mechanics. His teacher died and the school asked my dad to teach the rest of the class. He did such a good job that the principal wrote

A "Swallow" airplane, the 1920 model had a top speed of 85 mph.

letters and got him a little money to attend Western Michigan Teachers College (now Western Michigan University) in the southwestern peninsula. Dad graduated with a degree and became a teacher. When he had passed on, during my review of his papers I saw a paper showing his first-year annual salary as a teacher of auto mechanics—$1,700.

While he was going to college, he got a part-time job as an airplane mechanic. Then he started to fly airplanes, which in those days were made of wood frames covered with painted canvas. They had two wings placed above one another for lift and might on a good day do a hundred miles an hour. Dad and his pilot partner barnstormed around southern Michigan at the fairs and would take passengers up in the fore and aft two-seater while Dad stayed on the ground.

He told me a story about one time at Thanksgiving dinner he got into a fight with his brother about which was faster, my dad's plane, or his brother's Model A Ford. They decided to have a race the next day, from Escanaba to Gladstone. The only rule was Dad had to follow the road. They would start the race by Dad flying over his brother's car and dropping a handkerchief with a rock in it. Dad said that he was quite a way ahead, then he had to make a turn to the right. Suddenly his brother started gaining. My father had run into a strong headwind. His brother won, and Dad said he never let him forget it.

After he had passed on, I was able to collect several of the artifacts of his flying career: his flying goggles, several pictures of his crashes, his license as a certified airplane mechanic, a brochure for the type of plane he flew, a Swallow; a piece of the propeller that was left from one of his crashes (Dad crashed three times and survived), and some maps that he had used when he was flying.

Dad became the director of industrial training for the Battle Creek School System. He started the first practical nurse's training program and the first post-high school bricklayer's training program in the state. When he retired, the governor recognized him with a personal letter of commendation and thanks.

Being in charge of industrial training for the school system gave Dad license to visit the shops on the weekends. I remember him taking me as a kid to the shops on Saturdays and him telling and showing me about all the machines. Dad had his own woodshop in the basement and decided he was going to build a boat. To build a boat he had to design it and build plans. He laid out the boat in full scale on the living room floor with string. Then made his paper plans from the string layout. He then cut out of wood all of the parts and built the boat with clamps in the basement.

It had to be constructed with clamps in order to get it out of the house. He would have to take it apart and move it outside, but to where? We had a one-car garage. So, he built a second bay on the garage to house the boat. But he didn't have a motor. World War II had started and there were no motors available as everything was going toward the war effort. When the war was over, he got a motor. By then I was old enough to help him install the Gray Marine six-cylinder inboard engine. The boat was patterned after the Chris Craft wooden boats of the time, with lots of mahogany and varnish.

I remember when we launched the boat on her maiden voyage. As we motored across Gull Lake with my mother sitting in the back, Dad driving and me in the left seat, the boat started to slant down in the back. Dad asked me to look in the engine compartment back aft. I did, and water was pouring in. We were sinking! Dad turned around and hightailed it for the dock We barely made it and tied the boat up to the dock just in time. What we discovered the hard way was that you needed to soak a wooden boat for about two days before launching so the wood had time to swell up and close all the little gaps between planks.

Dad and I often went fishing in that boat. We would start on one side of the lake, drift across the lake as my father dozed to the other side and sometimes, I even caught a fish. We had to let them go however, as my mother wouldn't let us take the fish home. Cooking them, she said, would "smell up her kitchen."

My mother gave me many gifts, although at the time they didn't always seem like presents. One gift was that every night when I went to bed, I had to recite either the Lord's prayer or the 23rd Psalm and say my multiplication tables. That stopped when I was moved into the basement.

The basement consisted of a coal fed furnace, a fireplace, a pool table, and a coal bin. I got to know that coal bin well, because my job was to shovel coal into the furnace in the wintertime to heat the house. That was one of my many chores. Other furniture included my couch and a metal locker where I kept my clothes.

My remembrances of the basement were that I played a lot of pool, and of my father chasing me around the pool table when he was going to spank me with a stick when I got in trouble with my mother, which was several times a week. He did this for several years until I got big enough and finally told him he was not going to hit me again. He didn't. After Dad passed away, Marjorie took the pool table with her and had it totally restored. We subsequently played quite a few games later during one of my trips to Muskegon, Michigan on the lake where we held family reunions.

My mother insisted that a proper child "always opened doors for women and older people, took off his hat when inside, and spoke only when spoken to."

Later on, besides always having a job during the summer months, I had to go to the library and check out a book, read it, and then give her a written book-report. I generally did as I was told, and when I went to the library, I became intrigued with a series of books about submarines.

The books were written by the chief salvage officer of the Navy, Commander Edward Ellsberg. He wrote 18 books and retired in Maine after 30 plus years with the rank of a full admiral. I read all of his books and began collecting them.

Another gift that my mother gave me was an appreciation for music. She had an old upright piano in the living room, and she felt that I should learn how to play the piano. She gave me money to take the bus into town and go to the Congregational church where the director of music for the church gave music lessons on the side.

I started to go to the lessons where I practiced scales time after time, for hours on end. I would then have to practice at home in preparation for the next lessons. It got very boring so I figured out a better plan. I took the money and went into town but went to the movies instead. I saw every cowboy movie and was getting away with it.

I had been able to fool my mother when playing at home because for some reason, if I heard it, I could play it.

Then one day my mother asked, "When is your recital?"

"What's a recital?" I asked.

That was it, I was busted! I actually continued to play throughout my life and got good enough where I could play in piano bars in San Diego when my ship was back in the States. I had learned that there were two people in a bar that always met the women, the bartender and the piano player, and I could never remember how to mix all those drinks! I still play today on a beautiful baby grand piano that my kids gave me for my 50th birthday.

My mother always took care of me in spite of our many battles. I always had clean clothes and I always had three well cooked meals a day in spite of the fact that I always seemed to be hungry. When my mother baked, she always baked two pies, one for me and one for everybody else.

As I grew up, I went to school by walking more than a mile each way. I skipped the third grade, not because I was smarter than the other kids, simply because at eight, I was too big.

As I mentioned earlier, one of my mother's rules was that I always had to have a job in the summer. Whether it was having a paper route, working as a lifeguard at a local beach, or working as a dishwasher in a boy's camp, or mowing lawns, I had to have a job.

The only job I ever got fired from was working as a car-hop at a local Dairy Queen. Competition emerged from a new A&W built right across the street. The owner of the A&W hired good-looking girls in mini-skirts who served their food on roller skates.

"OK guys," our manager said one morning, "tomorrow you all need to show up with roller skates, you can all roller skate, can't you?"

I looked at my buddy, he grinned at me, and we both nodded our heads in the affirmative. The next day we showed up for work and I promptly fell down twice with a tray full of food, followed by me dumping a malted milk and hotdog all over a customer—in his car.

"Hale, you're fired!" was the next thing I heard.

The second job I had was as a camp counselor working in Peterborough, New Hampshire at the University of Massachusetts Sargent Camp. I had just graduated from high school and I had to work June and July before reporting to freshman football camp at the University of Michigan.

I got through the camp okay but decided to save the money I had made by hitchhiking back to Battle Creek, some 900 miles. That was a bit of an

adventure. I had my rolled-up sleeping bag, a backpack, and $200 hidden in my shoes.

I did well the first day, getting rides out of New England. I slept the first night in a field. The second day, though, I was in trouble. I got rides to the outskirts of Niagara Falls but it was raining and very cold as I arrived in the evening.

I called my folks from a phone booth (remember those?) as I knew Dad had a brother who lived in the city. Anyway, I hooked up with my uncle and spent the night sleeping at his house. The next morning, I asked him to drop me off at the bridge at the entrance to Canada, as going across that part of Canada would save me quite a lot of miles.

"Your folks don't know you are doing this," my uncle said as he dropped me off. "I have to let them know what you're doing."

"I understand, no problem," I said. "I should be home in a day or so. I'm going right across Canada and I will be in Michigan; I'll be all right. Thanks for all your help."

I walked across the bridge and went through the Canadian Customs, no problem. I was able to get rides across Canada, arriving at the US Customs on the entrance to Michigan. But they didn't want to let me in!

I don't know what the problem was. Yeah, I was a big guy, 17 years old with nothing but a backpack and a sleeping bag, seeking entrance to the United States with no identification. What's wrong with that?

They questioned me intensely about my story, I told them about where I lived, that Battle Creek was the home of Kellogg's, and that my family took the factory tour each month during WW II because we got a free variety pack that we ate for breakfast every day during the war. I guess that I convinced them, for they eventually let me in. I arrived a day later in Battle Creek with my $200 intact.

Later I found out that they were on the hunt for a killer who sort of fit my description! Glad I remembered that cereal!

As I mentioned earlier, I was supposed to report to freshman football practice at the University of Michigan. But I had had enough of school. It was boring for me, I didn't study, and graduated with a C average. Every report card had the same notation; "Dick could do so much better if he would only apply himself." My kids, during one of my much later birthday parties, presented me with some of my grades and gave me hell for always pushing them to get better grades. Oh well.

Going on to college in my mind meant four more years of sitting in a classroom being bored so I decided I wanted to go into the Navy. At 17, I had to have my parent's permission to join the Navy which they readily gave. My guess is that by that time, they had wondered what they had gotten themselves into. So, I joined the US Navy in late August of 1955 at age 17, one of those dumb executive decisions young people make.

It turned out to be the first great move of my career—a game-changer.

AT SEA

I went through basic training at Great Lakes Illinois Naval Training Center. Filled with ideas and dreams of glory from Commander Ellsberg, I tried to get into the submarine corps. They rejected me because I was too tall to fit inside a submarine.

But size did have its advantages. I was exempted from KP duty—peeling potatoes, doing dishes, and cleaning up the slop from the mess hall—because I played football for the training center's team, the Great Lakes Bluejackets.

We played the other military bases and some of the colleges in the area. I remember one game where we were playing the Air Force and I was getting the crap kicked out of me at left defensive end. I was in for a long afternoon. We didn't have any scouting reports, so I asked the coach who it was that I was facing.

"That's Lt. Ron Kramer, three-time All-American from Michigan serving out his military ROTC duty," the coach said with a smile. "He was just drafted by the Detroit Lions."

I was right, it was a long afternoon. But that was a low point. I had some good times at Great Lakes, although they weren't exactly respectable hijinks. Alcohol fueled many a spree, something that at the time I didn't consider.

Take the time John Cochran, who played tackle next to me, and I decided that we would go into Chicago to see what we could find—like girls. We were in uniform and started at the local USO where we got some free chow. We learned that they had a dance scheduled for later that evening so there was some hope. The USO was located right downtown in the middle of the "Loop" where all the restaurants, hotels and bars were located.

We couldn't get into a bar as we were both underage, but we found an old guy that agreed to buy us a bottle of booze if we gave him an extra five bucks. Remember, as seamen recruits we were at the lowest pay grade—$78 a month, free uniforms, a roof over our heads (the barracks) and three meals a day. That was it, so we were not rich by any means.

We decided to pool our money and get a room at the local YMCA hotel, which gave discounts to servicemen. Our plan was to go to the USO dance, meet some girls, stay the night in the hotel (unless we got a better offer) and then go back to the base on the train the next morning.

But then Big John and I got into the booze. We were both 18, had no experience drinking, but had a full fifth of cheap whisky in front of us. We got tanked up pretty quickly and then started showing each other the best way to block in football.

We were banging into the walls, knocked over the lamp several times, laughing and in general raising hell, and as it turns out, making a lot of noise. Big John got that name for a reason. He played tackle in the middle of the line for a reason. He went about six foot five and 260 pounds and when we hit something wrestling, it went down.

The phone rang.

It was the hotel manager complaining that we were making too much noise. We apologized and said we'd tone it down.

After a little while and another drink, we started wrestling again. Someone knocked on the door. It was the hotel manager!

I panicked. "Get rid of that bottle," I told John.

"Where?"

"Open the window and put it out on the window ledge."

Big mistake. The YMCA Hotel was built in a square with a patio in the middle. We were on the 12th floor.

Big John opened the window, put the almost empty bottle on the ledge and slammed the window back down, just as I opened the front door.

Just as the manager came into the room, the bottle reached the concrete patio after falling 12 stories and exploded. We were thrown out of the Chicago YMCA Hotel. We never made it to the USO dance and they probably wouldn't have let us in anyway.

We slept on benches at Union Train Station. The local cops often let servicemen in uniform sleep there as it was Chicago in November and it was cold outside. My 18th birthday was coming up on the 20th. I was establishing a pattern, a bad habit of letting my size, my love of violence, and drinking dominate me. I'm not sure if I thought about it in those terms, but a part of me knew I had to stop the destructive behavior.

* * *

At the end of basic training, all recruits had to report to the senior chief to get their assignments. I knocked on the door and the senior chief responded.

"Enter."

Upon entering I stood at attention.

"Seaman Hale," he barked. "Now that you have finished your basic training it is my understanding that you want to go to sea—is that right?"

“Yes sir.

“East Coast or West Coast?”

“I would like to be on the West Coast if that is possible, sir,” I piped up. The chief was scary.

“Seamen Hale I can get you on a ship next week but before I do that, I would like you to go over to the table in the corner and pick up that tool and repeatedly hit the iron plate on the table with the tool.”

Not really understanding, but not wanting to piss off a senior chief, a WWII veteran, and the guy that was going to get me on a ship, I complied. After several minutes of hitting the metal plate with my hammer, the Chief shouted at me to stop.

“Seaman Hale, I can get you on a ship next week, but you are going to wield that hammer chipping paint for the rest of your tour—or you are going to qualify for electronics school.”

“What’s electronics?”

The rest is history. It’s strange how a single moment in time can affect the direction of your entire life. I don’t remember the chief’s name but he saw something in me I had never seen in myself. He saw that I was more than a big guy with a quick step and a quicker temper. In that brief exchange, he set me on a path of success that I followed for the rest of my life.

Upon graduating from basic electronics school at Great Lakes, I was transferred to the USS *Pictor* AF 54 which was refueling at Pearl Harbor on its way to patrol off of the coast of Japan and Korea.

I was to take a train from Chicago to Alameda Naval Air Station in Oakland, California on the other side of the bay from San Francisco, then catch a naval transport plane to Pearl Harbor to report to the *Pictor*. As I had never been on a train or flown in an airplane, this was an adventure.

I arrived in Alameda and boarded the four-engine prop plane with my sea bag, a 30- by 48-inch-long sack that held everything I owned. We took off bound for Pearl. About 10 minutes from the point of no return—halfway—one of the engines caught fire. We were in danger of going down! Fortunately, the pilot and crew got the fire out and we returned to San Francisco flying on three engines. My first airplane flight could have been a short one.

Anyway, back in Alameda, I caught another plane two days later. I arrived in Pearl Harbor and walked down the pier with my sea bag on my shoulder just in time to catch my ship.

"Permission to come aboard?" I asked the duty sentry.

"Permission granted," was the response and I was on my first US Navy ship. We left Pearl the

The* Pictor*, in the center, replenishing the carrier* Yorktown *and destroyer* Bausell *in 1957.

next day to support the fleet currently on patrol off the coast of Korea. I was 18 years old.

The *Pictor* was a refrigerator ship whose mission was to supply goods to ships while underway. The replenishment process was tricky with two ships steaming in parallel about 100 feet apart while foodstuffs were "high-lined" across the 100 feet to the customer ship. Sometimes bodies were high-lined back to us as we were a refrigerator ship capable of storing the remains.

I was 18 years old. I remained on the *Pictor* as part of the fire control gang who were responsible for keeping the radar for the guns and other weapons working. I was assigned to the radar part of the crew. I remained on the *Pictor* for about one year and then was transferred to the USS *Jason*, a heavy-repair ship which was operating in the Sea of Japan.

The *Jason* was big but slow. It was heavily armed with eight 5-inch guns plus four 40-mm anti-aircraft guns, a bunch of 20-mm machine guns, a

USS* Jason *AR-8 heavy repair ship

long-distance search radar and two fire control radars, one for the forward battery and one for the aft guns. I was assigned to the radar crew.

My boss, rated a first class fire-control technician, was a guy by the name of Richard Davidson. Dick was a big guy and a WWII vet. He had served on the USS *California*, which was sunk during the Japanese sneak attack on Pearl Harbor, December 7, 1941.

Before my first inspection, I got ready by polishing my shoes and belt buckle, getting a haircut, and pressing my uniform. Dick did nothing.

He was very overweight and had his T-shirt and gut hanging out over his belt. In general he looked like a slob. Because he was tall, I always stood next to him. I figured his appearance would take some of the pressure off of me.

The fleet commodore and his junior officers and clerks approached, inspected me, and wrote me up for my shoes not being shiny enough. Then they moved on to Dick. I thought all hell was about to break loose, but the commodore looked at Dick.

"Please shake my hand, sailor," the officer said. The inspection crew then moved on without any comment. Dick just smiled and I was flabbergasted.

After the inspection was over, I asked Dick how he got away with it. Dick laughed.

"After I survived the sinking of the *California*, I was transferred to a heavy cruiser and that got shot out from under me too during the battle of Midway. Then they put me on a tin can (a destroyer) and that was sunk."

Dick said he thought he had spent more time in the water than he had on land. When the inspecting officer saw all of Dick's medals, he just wanted to thank him for his service to his country.

Dick stayed in the Navy and eventually retired. Several years later I ran into Dick, who was driving a taxicab, happy as a clam and glad to be back with his wife and kids. He is one of my heroes.

I remember being caught in a typhoon, as a hurricane was called in that part of the world, off the coast of Subic Bay in the Philippines. My watch station in a storm condition on the *Jason* was up in the fire control turret, the highest point on the ship. Think about the crow's nest from "Moby Dick" or something. The waves were about 60 feet from the waterline. When we went down into the trough of the oncoming wave, I looked up at the crest of the oncoming wave. If we lost power and steerage it was all over. I was too dumb and inexperienced to understand that then, but I do still remember those waves.

I spent Christmas and Thanksgiving dinners aboard the *Jason* patrolling the Straits of Taiwan while Chinese fighters buzzed us. We were at battle stations for what seemed like forever.

* * *

The first time I got into trouble while in the Navy was in Long Beach, California. After three days, the ship had survived a typhoon but had suffered some damage We were ordered back to the states for repairs at a shipyard in Long Beach. I was on liberty with a few buddies and as usual we headed for a bar. We drank some beer, chased some women (didn't catch any) and decided to walk back to the ship. As we turned the corner, my two buddies and I saw the Long Beach Police dragging by his heels a shipmate who had apparently passed out in a bar. His head was bumping along the sidewalk and he was being treated very badly so we offered to the police to take him back to the ship.

They told us to disperse.

We made the offer again.

"Disperse."

We turned away and started back to the shipyard which was about a mile away.

"Get the big guy," I heard one of the cops say. I guess that was me because the next thing I knew three cops were grabbing me. I fought back and that made them beat me even more. I was dragged to the paddy wagon where our shipmate was housed. The police then took us on a little ride, what they call "diesel therapy." There was nothing inside the paddy wagon to hold on to as the driver repeatedly accelerated then slammed on the brakes. We were getting busted up pretty good. After a while we were transferred to a holding cell at the Long Beach Police Department.

An officer from our ship was the senior officer on shore patrol duty that night and had seen the whole thing. He made some calls and we were released into the custody of the Shore Patrol and driven to the ship, where we were bandaged up at sickbay. No charges were made and the whole thing was over.

* * *

Those scars have long healed, but I carry with me a memory that still comes back in the dark moments and small hours of my life. A Navy shipmate of mine, a buddy, was killed and I was witness to his death. His last words on this earth were, "Don't leave me."

I didn't leave him, and I haven't since. I volunteered to accompany his remains back to his hometown in Ohio.

Ten days after his death, sitting in the club car with a Makers on the rocks in hand, I let the bumpety-bump, bumpety-bump of the train wheels lull me to rest. For two days I heard that sound and for two days I had been thinking back to all that had happened and forward to what lay ahead.

My friend's casket and I were due at the Columbus station in three hours. The plan was to hook up with the funeral director around 10:30 at night. The brass had contacted the local Naval Reserve unit and they had agreed to provide the pallbearers, honor guard, and a bugler. I had an American flag that had been signed by all of the crew. It would cover my friend's coffin.

"Another Maker's," I belched as the steward walked by. As the waiter left, I finished the drink I had and offered a quiet prayer and toast to my friend.

He was a second-class petty officer in the US Navy and was only 22 years old. I would miss him. I turned my head to the window and cried, glad that only the steward would see my tears.

The train stopped and the honor guard came up to the baggage car. The men were all in uniform and stood at attention despite the late hour. Many of them probably had kids or wives or had rushed to the station from work. Yet they chose to honor one of their own. They were great. The coffin was slid out and carried to the funeral director's hearse by the honor guard. They treated the coffin—and me—with profound respect.

"You must be tired, tomorrow will be a busy day," said the funeral director. "Let's go over the details while I drive you to your hotel."

He went over the details of the funeral as I tried to stay awake.

"As far as tomorrow goes, the funeral starts at two o'clock with the military pallbearers. The Honor Guard will fire three volleys and the bugler will play Taps. You'll say a few words, the flag covering the casket will be folded, given to you, and you will deliver the flag to the parents."

It was raining when the funeral director dropped me off at the hotel. The bad weather continued into the next day, which was overcast, gray, and cool.

The uniformed pall bearers carried my friend's flag-draped coffin from the limo to the burial plot. Rows of relatives, friends, and family were seated across from where I stood at attention in my dress uniform, awaiting the slow procession of the pall-bearers and the casket.

USS Elkhorn AF 8 at pier in Pearl Harbor

The mournful sound of the bugler playing Taps followed. The honor guard fired off three rounds in salute. The flag on the coffin, the one from me and the boys from the *Jason*, was folded and presented to me. I turned stiffly to my friend's mom and dad.

"Please accept this flag in honor of your son on behalf of a grateful nation," I said.

Suddenly the sun broke through the overcast. It all seemed almost inappropriate. The day was a long one, filled with many memories and much sadness.

* * *

I did three deployments on the *Jason* then was transferred to the US *Elkhorn*, homeported in Pearl Harbor. I was by now the senior fire control technician aboard, the same rank as my hero, Dick Davidson, equivalent to a sergeant in the Army and thus an NCO responsible for how well the radar-controlled guns preformed. After the annual firing exercises the ship received the E for excellence. As a recipient you were allowed to paint the E on your ship. The *Elkhorn* had never received such an honor. The captain was so happy he offered to recommend me for officers candidate school. I was intrigued, but also admitted that I didn't know where I wanted to go. Applying for officers school would commit me for another four years and I was not sure I wanted to make the Navy a career. He gave me some time to make up my mind, which I appreciated.

I resumed my love of surfing that I had developed while serving on the *Jason* off the shores of San Diego. I met a few of the native Hawaiians surfing and one in particular became a long-term friend.

There was a place called "Leroy's" on Ala Moana Boulevard on the outskirts of Honolulu, where I ended up one Saturday afternoon. There was a guy sitting at the bar and we were the only people there. We started talking.

"I'm not sure if you are a sailor, a tourist, or a beach bum," he joked.

"I am the first, feel like the second, but bordering on the third," I said.

We both laughed and then shot some pool at one of the tables in the back of the bar. His name was Mercer King, but everybody local knew him as "Sonny." We didn't know it at the time, but we were about to become life-long friends until he passed away in a hospital in Nashua, New Hampshire.

Sonny smoked incessantly and drank seven-and-seven's. I drank anything I could afford. We would spend a lot of life sailing and drinking in Hawaii, California, and New Hampshire.

Sonny took me to all the local hotspots. We chased visiting schoolteachers in Honolulu (came close a couple of times but didn't catch any) and generally did what young single men do. My ship went to sea from time to time, but his was the first phone call I made when we got back into port.

Sonny was running a small business with a few employees so our shenanigans were generally on the weekends. We shot a lot of pool, drank a lot, and Sonny taught me how to play chess, a game I still play today, some 60 years later.

After two years, I was transferred back to Great Lakes, and we had to say goodbye. Not easy for us as we enjoyed each other's company and had experienced a lot of good times together. We had become friends.

I had a shipmate on the *Elkhorn* who lived off board. His wife had followed him to Pearl so they lived in Navy housing on the base. He approached me one day and said that his wife had a friend from San Jose, California who was visiting. Would I be interested in going to dinner with them? I lived on board the ship and was single and horny so that was a no-brainer.

That's how I met Andrea, the woman I would marry. Meeting her was a high point of my final tour of sea duty. The low moment, not surprisingly, involved too much alcohol. While on the island of Midway—yes, the famous island of the famous WW II battle, I had my second brush with Navy discipline.

We had pulled into Midway to offload aviation fuel. When offloading fuel, it was customary to grant liberty to half of the crew to reduce annihilation of the full ship's complement if something went wrong. The gasoline tankers were very dangerous and if you were assigned to one of them you drew hazardous duty pay.

I was assigned shore leave and went to the NCO club with a few buddies. We drank beer, played shuffleboard, or shot pool from about 2 p.m. until 8 that evening. It was dark when I staggered out of the club but I could see what I thought were the red aircraft warning lights on the mast of my ship.

I kept my eyes, which were not focusing that well, on the lights and headed directly for them. It seemed like I had been walking a long time and not making much progress.

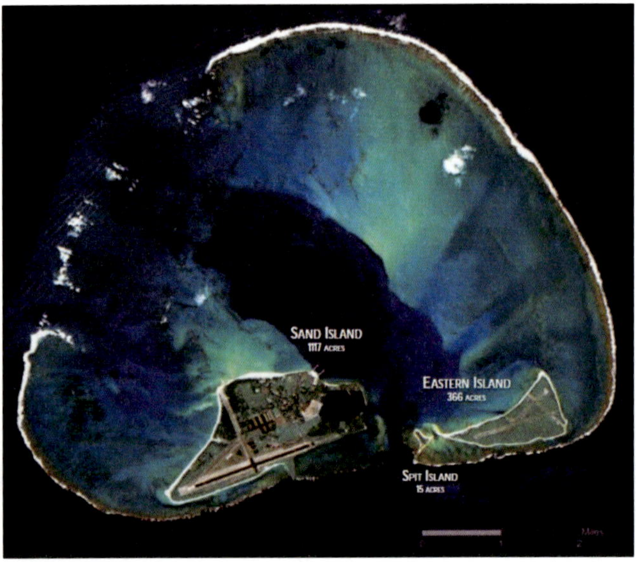

Satellite image of Midway Atoll

Then I spotted a bike leaning up against a building and decided that a bike was better than walking.

But on Midway the only cars belonged to the Shore Patrol and bikes were considered cars, so stealing a bike was like stealing a car. I was only borrowing the bike, I thought, as I wobbled down the road, eyes fixed on what I thought were my ship's red aircraft warning lights on the mast. Finally I reached a paved road and started making good time. Suddenly a bright light came on behind me!

I was about to discover that I was actually on a runway with a plane about to land and that the red lights were actually at the airport. I swerved the bike off the runway into the bingo ditch, which was used to accumulate all of the rainwater and dirt from the runway.

I had sort of a crash. Actually I was a mess, covered with mud and who knows what. I know it really smelled! The next thing I knew was that I was being escorted back to the ship with my hands handcuffed behind me. Upon arriving at the ship, I again requested permission to come aboard and the officer of the deck paused, signed some papers, then granted permission.

I was then escorted down below, to the brig. The captain ordered thirty days' suspension aboard ship, which was particularly painful as the ship was headed to Hong Kong for R&R. If anything, the experience made a decision for me; maybe I shouldn't apply for officers' school.

SILICON VALLEY

Having six years of sea duty on my record gave me a lot of seniority so I requested shore duty as I was about to be married. I was then assigned to the Great Lakes Training Center in Illinois, the same base where I went through basic training, as an instructor.

I still had two years left on my enlistment. Andrea and I were married in St Joseph's Church in San Jose, then were to drive over the Rocky Mountains to Great Lakes where I would report for duty. At the wedding, Andrea as the bride had several hundred people on the left side of the aisle. On my side of the aisle was one couple, a distant cousin and her husband whom I did not even remember ever meeting. It looked so weird that after a while the ushers started seating people over on the groom's side.

The drive, in Andrea's 1956 2-door Chevy, was an adventure. Andrea got very sick and ended up permanently losing her hearing in one ear. We lived in Navy housing which was a two-room unit plus a bathroom apartment in a converted barracks.

Shortly after the marriage, Andrea became pregnant and nine months later David was born in a Navy hospital. He cost $50, a story I still like to remind him of. I still recall the 2 a.m. feedings, warming the bottles of Simulac, and cradling David as I walked around lulling him back to sleep.

While at sea on my three ships, I took an electrical engineering correspondence course from Capital Radio Engineering Institute. I had discovered a direct linkage between studying engineering, rank advancement, money, and beer. All jokes aside, my mother's emphasis on studying had begun to pay off. I saw the value of learning. I graduated from CREI after six years and a lot of beer. I was assigned to teach radar theory at Great Lakes. I started going to the University of Illinois nights and weekends, studying electrical engineering. I also worked part-time as a janitor at a local publishing house to make a few extra bucks.

I taught radar theory for two years and when the two years were finished, I had a major decision to make. My tour of duty was complete and I had to either reenlist and go back out to sea or get out of the Navy.

Andrea's family was from San Jose, about 35 miles from Stanford and on a trip to visit them I had applied for a job at Stanford that they were advertising in the local newspaper. Stanford had invited me to take an engineering test and offered me a job when I got out of the service. They had a major project in process, building the three-mile-long Linear Nuclear Accelerator.

I had a one-year-old son, was married, and now had a firm job offer to work at Stanford University.. During my six years of sea duty I often saw the stress that families endured while the parent was on deployment. So I decided to take care of my family and get out of the Navy.

A little problem arose, however, during my check out process. A routine chest X-ray showed spots all over my lungs so I was immediately admitted to the Navy Hospital at Great Lakes. I was only 27 years old and was being wheeled into a ward for people who didn't come back alive.

The first diagnosis was lymphoma. In 1964 there was no known cure for lymphoma and you generally were gone within 12 to 24 months. Many tests later, including a chest biopsy, they changed the diagnosis to Boecks Sarcoidosis, a very rare disease of the lymph nodes which had no known cause or cure. The Navy convened a medical review board and declared my condition to be Navy-related, which allowed me to be treated by the VA. I was followed by the VA for several years, but the

Sarcoid went dormant, and the VA was useless anyway, so I quit going.

I resigned from the Navy and was honorably discharged after nine years of service as a fire control technician first class. I had passed the chief's exam in the upper three percent and would have made chief if I stayed in. But sea duty was deadly for families, so I took my family to California and went to work at Stanford University as a junior engineer. It was August of 1964.

* * *

Stanford was my first real job. We were designing and building the most powerful magnifying glass in the world. I was being paid $10,000 a year which, after my Navy experience, seemed to me like all the money in the world. Life was great!

An accelerator shoots a powerful electro-magnetic radio frequency beam of energy into materials and explodes the material at the sub-atomic level. The accelerator was three miles long, built in ten-

Stanford Linear Accelerator, shown in an aerial digital orthoimage. The two roads seen near the accelerator are California Interstate 280 to the east and Sand Hill Road due northwest.

foot sections with 84 microwave cavities in each 10-foot section. There was a hole the size of a dime in the center of each cavity through which the high energy electron beam passed. Through that process scientists hope to find new particles other than electrons, protons, and neutrons.

Dr. Wolfgang Panofsky

Each section was on a bed that could be adjusted in two dimensions.

The alignment was a critical parameter. I found it curious that the federal Department of Atomic Research had chosen to build this super sensitive accelerator on top of the San Andreas earthquake fault, which ran right through the site. Our taxpayer's money at work, I guess.

Dr. Wolfgang Panofsky was the director of the project and I was at a level four layers down from him although I did get to meet him. Two men were killed on the site while I was there in bizarre accidents. One died when a metal locker fell over him in the locker room as another worker was climbing a ladder leaned against the other side.

The Linear Accelerator was built in an underground tunnel with shielded sides, as the radiation levels became very high due to the energy being pumped into the tube every 20 feet to further energize the beam. A huge tractor digger was used to dig the trench. The digger had rubber tires higher than a man's head. As the digger was moving, the driver raised the digging arm and hit the high-tension wires powering the whole project. The electricity jumped the tire and grounded through the body of a worker walking alongside the digger. Bizarre and tragic!

After a year of design work, we were into a production mode as we built the ten-foot sections. My primary engineering work was done and I began looking for other opportunities in a field I had grown to love.

I interviewed at a company in Santa Clara south of Stanford much closer to home, again as a junior engineer, and was made an offer working in the engineering department.

* * *

At Western Microwave Laboratories my new boss was Bob Addington, senior VP of engineering. I actually took a small cut in pay to join Western as

Prototype of Lunar Excursion

I was very impressed by Addington during the interview and felt that I would learn a lot from him.

Over the next two years I was assigned several projects including a building a component for the Lunar Excursion Module, the "go-kart" used during one of the first landings on the moon. Thc prototype is currently in the Smithsonian in Washington. I also worked on the S-band transmitter that sent data back to earth.

After about two years Bob Addington approached me and stated that he was going to leave Western Microwave Labs to start his own company. Would I like to join him as one of the founders?

I told him that I was honored but didn't have any money but if he was still interested, I would be proud to join him. On January 1 of 1967 we started Addington Laboratories. When I gave my notice at

Western, Ted Geisler, the company president, offered me a deal: if at any time within one year, I wanted to come back to Western, they would guarantee me a job and reimburse me for any money I had invested in Addington. I thought that was a pretty unique letter. I never went back.

* * *

Over the next 10 years we built Addington Laboratories up to several hundred employees and then sold the company to the Eaton Corporation, a large public company.

During those 10 years I had acquired some stock, and rose from the engineering ranks, to become vice president and chief operating office of the whole company. One of the projects that we developed was an exciter for a high-powered radar jammer for the Navy.

In the early stages of the Vietnam war, the US was losing a high number of aircraft due to their being shot down by SAMs (Surface to Air) missiles. The Navy issued an expedited contract for the development of a radar jammer.

The SAMs were beam riders, which meant the Navy bomber was illuminated by the ground-based radar and the missile followed the beam into the target. We needed a jammer that could fool or jam the enemy radar. The government issued contracts to

Raytheon and Hughes Aircraft. We became the sole contractor to both of them. I always felt a special kind of pressure because if we failed Navy pilots would die.

This jammer went into a retrofitted EA6B Navy bomber where all the armament was removed from the plane and replaced with electronics. The mission for the EA6B as a standoff jammer was to jam the ground-based radar and thus let the bombers and fighters go in and take out the SAM sites and other strategic and tactical targets.

Reports came back that the kill ratio of our US planes went way down as a result of the EA6B effort. This effort was one of the first products of the newly emerging electronic warfare component of how our troops went to war.

* * *

On the home front, Andrea and I had a second child, Laura. She definitely cost me more than $50 but Laura was worth it. Andrea and I had lost a child and Laura's was a breech birth, so we both were scared. I recall praying in the chapel of the hospital as Andrea braved a long and difficult delivery. Laura and her older brother David remain the pride of my life.

As I had come up through the ranks and made more money at Addington, we moved from our first

900-square-foot house which I bought for $9,000. I painted the house, built a shed, put in a paved driveway and sold it two years later for $13,000.

I took the proceeds and bought our second home, a much larger one in Campbell, California. After another two years, our next-door neighbor made me an offer.

"Dick as you know my wife just passed away and I want to sell my house to change my environment," he said. "Do you want to buy the house? It might be nice for you as I see you have two young kids."

He had the same house as we did except his had an inground swimming pool and was on a corner lot.

"I would love to, but the only way I could afford it is if I could keep my existing house, rent it out and use the proceeds to help pay for yours." I told him.

We made a deal, and I bought the corner house with the pool. A few years later, I sold both houses, and bought what would now be called an estate in the upscale, beautiful town of Los Gatos. The house had a large in-ground pool, 13 different species of fruit trees, and a gorgeous view from a hill overlooking Los Gatos and what was starting to be known as Silicon Valley.

One day we were out at the swimming pool. Laura was challenged by a cousin to race to the end of the pool. Being too much like me, she accepted the challenge. They started, and all the way down the pool, with every stroke, she looked up at me, fierce and proud, her little face gleaming, to see if I was looking. That image still pulls at my heart.

Remember I mentioned the boat I helped my father build? My son and I built a small wooden boat in the shop together. We labored away, built the boat, and tied the eight-foot boat to the top of the car. As we drove to the lake, the boat came loose from the top of the car, flew over into the other oncoming lane and it was hit by a very large semi-truck and trailer. When we stopped, and looked for the boat, there was nothing left—nothing.

I bought a 90 percent finished boat a few days later.But I still have the image of that boat flying up in the air and the look on my son's face when we found the remains.

* * *

I ran with an eclectic mix of engineers and oddballs. Alcohol was usually at the center of our gatherings, particularly at a place called The Live Oak Inn located in the heart of Los Gatos. A bunch of us used to meet for drinks and lunch every Saturday afternoon.

We shot the bull and watched football. I recall that one Saturday one of the guys was complaining about his wife's cat.

"That damn cat pees all over the rug, and the place smells like shit," he said.

"That's nothing," another guy stated. "My wife has this little poodle and he shits all over the lawn, and I'm the one that has to clean it up."

This went on for a while and finally a guy named Gary Dahl chimed in.

"That's nothing, I have a pet rock."

"A pet rock, what the hell is that?" one of us asked.

Gary, an unemployed advertising executive whose wife was working in the bar as a waitress, said, "Yeah, it never shits or pisses, it doesn't eat much, there are no doctor bills, and it never talks back."

Everybody started laughing so hard we were about to be thrown out of the place. Thus, was born The Pet Rock. Gary was to sell over a million Pet Rocks in the four months before Christmas.

Soon he had every unemployed housewife in Los Gatos looking for rocks in Los Gatos creek. He put together a booklet titled, "The Care and Feeding of Your Pet Rock." It came in a box with straw in the bottom and holes in the side so that your rock could breathe. Gary went from a down and out unemployed advertising executive to a multi-millionaire in just a few months.

Carrie Nation

He was smart enough to realize that this was just a fad, so he did two things. One, he researched the history of Los Gatos, and found out that nobody had ever gone broke owning a bar. So with his new-found wealth he bought a bar. He totally renovated the place, hired a bunch of buxom girls to be bartenders and waitresses, and renamed the bar "Carrie Nations."

Carrie Nation was a very active member and leader of the Temperance League before Prohibition. Definitely, a force to be reckoned with, she was known to attack bars with a hatchet, all the while singing and praying.

Gary established the motto: "Temperance with Moderation." He then emblazoned the motto on everything in the bar—napkins, menus, signs, and especially the T-shirts of all employees.

The second thing he did was sell the Pet Rock business. Verifying the existence and veracity of the greater fool theory, he actually found a buyer! As they concluded the deal over lunch and drinks at the Live Oak Inn, the somewhat tipsy new owner had a question: What are you going to do now with all that money?"

"I'm going to walk down to the Ferrari dealer at the end of the street, and buy me a new car," Gary, also somewhat tipsy, replied. "I've always dreamed about owning a Ferrari."

"I'll walk down with you; I've always wanted to see one up close," the new owner replied.

So the two of them staggered down to the end of the block and into the dealership. The salesman rushed over to Gary as he was now famous.

"Mr. Dahl, how may I help you?"

"I'd like to buy that black Ferrari that you have in the window, how much is it?"

"It's around $300,000," the salesman said, "but for you I could probably get it down to $295,000. Are you interested?:"

"I'll take it."

The new owner of the Pet Rock company who had been watching what was going on spoke up.

"Shit, I think I'd like to buy one too, except I want red," he said. "Can you do that?"

The salesman skeptically looked at the new guy.

"Yeah, yeah, who's going to pay for it?" said the salesman.

"You got lunch, I'll pay for them both," Gary said, and that's how Gary Dahl bought two Ferrari's on the same day. The Live Oak Inn subsequentially renamed the men's bathroom, "The Gary Dahl Room." The Live Oak Inn no longer exists, and Gary died in 2015. A true story, I was there.

The yin of the pet rock story is a study of the momentary integration of humor, courage, imagination, a respect for history, and native intelligence. The yang of the pet rock story is why, with those natural talents and skills, Gary's wife was working as a waitress, while Gary hung out in bars. Silicon Valley was gearing up, unemployment was low, and opportunities were all over the place. On the other hand, Gary made more money in six months than most men make in their entire life and Gary ended up being a storybook hero. Yet I wonder. Perhaps more a question than a lesson.

* * *

One of the engineers that worked at Addington was a guy named Bert. He was a somewhat crusty old guy who had decided to get an education at age 50. Bert got into Stanford, and got a bachelor's, master's, and PhD in electrical engineering without stopping. Bert was married but his wife was pretty sick and so he had hired a German lady as a live-in to take care of her. This she had done for almost 20 years.

Anyway, after we sold Addington, Bert was asked to stay on staff. A year later I was in New Hampshire running Omni Spectra and I got a call from Bert.

"Dick, I've got a problem and I don't know what to do."

"What's the problem?"

Bert said Vivian had passed away, and Annie, the live-in helper, had nowhere to go. Now Bert's so-called friends and neighbors were starting to talk. Bert never told me how old he was, but I guessed he was in his early seventies, as was Annie. He couldn't kick her out of the house after almost 20 years. Annie, an immigrant from Germany, had nowhere to go, and no source of income other than what Bert had paid her over the years.

I offered him a job in New Hampshire at the Merrimack plant. If he showed up with Annie no-one would know that they weren't married except me and I wasn't talking.

Bert sold his house in Palo Alto and moved out to New Hampshire with Annie. Bert never told me what happened if anything, but two years later he called me again.

"Dick, for estate reasons I think I should marry Annie," he said. "But I don't want it to get into the newspapers as some of our neighbors read that stuff and everybody thinks we are already married."

I thought about it for a moment.

"Bert, I'm a justice of the peace in the state of New Hampshire due to another adventure (don't ask!) and I can marry you legally," I proposed. "We could have the ceremony here at my house and nobody will be the wiser."

"OK."

I planned a ceremony in which I would say a few words, they would say their vows, and I would pronounce them man and wife. My son, David, would then push the button on the phonograph and play "The Wedding Song." David punched the wrong button, and "The Stars and Stripes Forever" roared out over the loudspeakers.

Wrong button—that was from our 4th of July party. It startled the hell out of everybody, then we all fell down from laughing so hard.

That was Bert and Annie's wedding and they lived happily together for another two years before Bert passed. Annie followed him within a year. They were my friends, and I often think fondly about both of them.

* * *

One day after work I stopped into a place in Santa Clara California called The Golden Pheasant. I sat down at the bar, ordered a drink, and looked down at the only other guy in the joint. He looked vaguely familiar.

"Sonny?"

He looked up.

"Dick?"

Thus, a reunion ensued. What are the odds of that happening? It was Sonny from Pearl Harbor.

Sonny, now called Merc after his full real name Mercer King, had moved to the mainland from his place in the islands and was working at the Ford Motor plant in Mountain View, California a few miles north of Santa Clara.

We hung out together for the next 10 years playing pool and chess. We also sailed together. I had told Merc that I had sailed once while in the Navy in a small boat, had loved it, and now wanted to learn how to sail. Merc wondered if there was somewhere we could take lessons.

I went into a bookstore and bought a book on how to sail. All we needed now was a boat. I bought my first sailboat, called a Lido 14. It was orange, used, and I thought the prettiest boat I could afford.

We took the trailable boat to some of the local lakes and practiced sailing. We spent a lot of time on the boat, thought we were pretty good, so decided to enter a local race. We were hot! Actually, by the time we finished the race, the race committee had pulled up stakes and gone home! Maybe we needed to learn something about racing.

We practiced a lot more, I studied racing tactics, and by the end of the year, we won the San Jose Sailing Club's Championship for the Lido Class boats.

Merc loved to fish, so one Saturday he convinced me to go with him to a local lake. It was very hot and after about three hours of no fish, not even a bite, we were laying by our poles when suddenly Merc's bobber went under.

He jumped up and hauled on his pole so hard the bobber and a four-inch bluegill went sailing out of the water, over our heads, and into a tree behind us.

I congratulated Merc on catching a giant fish. He looked at me and started climbing the tree to retrieve his catch. We drank a couple more beers until he said he was tired of me giving him shit about his giant catch so we went home. I still chuckle when I think of him climbing that tree!

* * *

I was extremely fortunate to have spent the first 13 years of my engineering and business career in the center of what we now know as Silicon Valley.

When I left the Navy and went to work at Stanford University's Linear Accelerator Center in 1964, I was smack dab in the center of it all.

Stanford University's Engineering Department was in effect the epicenter.

Graduates and attendees of that esteemed department founded companies like Hewlett-Packard, Varian, Watkins Johnson, Intel, Apple, Fairchild, and on and on. There was a business group called WEMA, the Western Electronics Manufacturers Association, that later became the American Electronics Association or AEA, that helped these companies mature along the way.

A restaurant/bar in Santa Clara called Renzo's was one of the central places everybody hung out. At lunch time, you could see David Packard drive into the parking lot in an old beat-up Chevy and Jerry Sanders founder of AMD (Advanced Micro Devices) who in those days was just starting up and didn't have a pot to piss in, drive in with his Rolls Royce.

"I have the whole history of Silicon Valley outlined on my tablecloths," Lorenzo Pieatro, the owner of the restaurant, told me one day. "Formulas, flow diagrams, plans, everything."

He was probably right.

Lorenzo made a lot of money but once a year he gave some back. He held an invitation-only special event for his regular patrons where he served a breakfast at the restaurant about 5:30 in the morning. Then guests were bused up to San Francisco for a fishing excursion beyond the Golden Gate Bridge. Lunch was served on board the boat and about 4 p.m. guests were bused back to the restaurant in Santa Clara.

At 7 p.m. Lorenzo then served up a six-course meal for the invitees. It was a black-tie dinner and was well-attended as it was considered an honor to be invited.

That was a magical time and place back then in the Sixties and Seventies. Innovation, creativity, thinking out of the box was the order of the day. In fact, Stanford added a course called "Thinking out of the Box." It was an exciting time. I have never worked so hard in my life. Men worked 12-hour days then went to a bar to have a drink and relax before going home.

It was a man's world and we abused our family relationships, our friends, our health, just about everything important in life, chasing the dream of being the next best thing. Patent and corporate lawyers made fortunes as they were all on the inside track of intellectual property gravy. People were at a premium, especially engineers, and salaries escalated out of control. The farmers that owned all of the apricot farms sold out to make room for Apples, IBMs and other centers of the growing industry.

Crazy times, and crazy people, and I loved it!

DUE EAST

We sold Addington Laboratories in 1977 after 10 years of profitable growth. I was still only 40 years old, had made some money, but was now out of a job. Several months later, as I was sitting on the porch of our home in Los Gatos, the phone rang. It was the president of Omni Spectra Corporation, one of the largest and oldest companies in our industry, a company much larger than Addington.

The president of Omni said that my reputation was one of fixing problems and growing electronic companies. He said that he had a problem and wondered if I would be willing to fly out to Omni Spectra's headquarters in New Hampshire to meet with him.

It was March, and I was outside in my shorts and T-shirt in Los Gatos, so I wasn't enthusiastic about flying to New Hampshire where it was snowing. I needed something to do, however, so I said yes. Omni was a publicly-owned company and traded on the NASDAQ exchange. Public companies are a whole different breed, with financial market-induced stresses and dynamics that are not always good for the long-term health of the company.

What I would learn is that public investors have very little allegiance to a company, and the pressures of the need for quarterly earnings growth can create short-term thinking by management at the expense of long-term investments that could ensure the growth and health of the company.

Omni was a large company with plants in New Hampshire, Massachusetts, Arizona, and England.

When I arrived in New Hampshire I met with Bevin Cherot, the president, who explained his problem (he actually had several). He suggested that I visit each of his plants and verify his problem and see if I could recommend a solution.

I agreed, as he was paying me and all my expenses, so I took the next 30 days and visited each of the plants. I did all the factory tours, talked with employees at several levels, management, and went to all the bathrooms.

The bathrooms? You would be surprised what you can learn by simply reading what's written on the bathroom walls above the urinals!

When I got back to New Hampshire I met with the president again and he asked me if I knew what the problems were.

I did.

He then asked me then if I knew how to fix the problems.

"Yes."

After a slight pause he asked me if I wanted the job.

I replied, "No."

He then made me an offer that I could not turn down. So I sold my home in Los Gatos, California and moved my family to New Hampshire. The prestige of joining Omni Spectra as a vice president plus the money was a compelling argument.

But Omni Spectra as a public company was in trouble. There were two major problems at the corporate level besides some operational problems at two of the four plants.

The company was founded in Detroit, Michigan and was unionized as a small component of the United Autoworkers union. As the union continually sought to raise wages, Omni was gradually pushed into an untenable competitive position. Efforts to reach an agreement with the union were not successful.

Omni was faced with only a few choices: move out of the state, close down, or sell the company. Omni decided to move to New Hampshire where a strong pro-business climate existed. But the move was poorly planned and executed. The company lost many of its most experienced workers and soon was tottering on the brink of bankruptcy.

The second thing Omni did that hurt its position was acquire its major competitor; a company called Americon. As part of the acquisition, Bevin Cherot, Americon's founder and president had become president of the new combined company. That's who hired me.

What I did not know was that the Omni Spectra board of directors did not like or trust Bevin. In fact, six months after I joined the firm the board of directors fired him and appointed a long time VP and general manager of the Omni Spectra Arizona plant as the new president.

Soon after joining the company, I was interviewed by the *Wall Street Journal*.

"Contrast the differences between the newly emerging Silicon Valley in California and the business environment in New Hampshire,". The reporter asked me. The interview was published in the *Journal* about a week later. I immediately got a bunch of calls from my friends in California. They were all a little upset as, apparently, I had been a little hard on California by contrasting the smog, increasing traffic, and the rapidly-increasing cost of housing with the pristine New Hampshire environment and cost of living.

Gov. Meldrim Thomson

"Mr. Hale you have a call," my secretary announced two days after the article surfaced.

"Take a note and tell whoever it is I will call them back in about 30 minutes," I said. I was right in the middle of a meeting. But she buzzed back in.

"I think you better take this call!" she replied.

"Dammit I am really busy, who is it?"

"It's the governor!"

The governor was Meldrim Thomson, who had been the governor of New Hampshire for a long time. He was very conservative and very tough, so I took the call!

He invited me to breakfast at his private home in Concord, New Hampshire, the state capital, as he refused to live in the governor's mansion. He was also the only governor in the US who ordered all the flags in the state lowered to half-mast when President Jimmy Carter gave away the Panama Canal. I had never even spoken to a governor before so of course I accepted his invitation.

A week later I showed up at his house at 8 a.m. and was greeted at the door by his wife, Anne. She ushered me into the kitchen where she was cooking blueberry pancakes. I was on time but the last to get there.

Seated around the table was Ross Tait, president of Ingersoll Rand; Herm Pouliot, publisher of the *Nashua Telegraph,* the largest newspaper in the State; Jack Bowers, a former undersecretary of the Navy and president of Sanders Associates, the largest company in the state; and the governor.

The governor's wife asked me how many pancakes did I want. The breakfast conversation then centered around my article and how we could make New Hampshire even more open for business. Toward the end of the breakfast I asked the governor, "As a newcomer to the state, how does one tell the difference between a hill and a mountain?"

"The same difference as between a pond and a lake," he responded. New England humor! That was the end of the breakfast and I never spoke to the governor again. He was finally voted out of office after three terms. He was the first of three governors I met during my 17 years in New Hampshire. What can I say? It's a small state.

* * *

As head of one of the larger companies in the state of New Hampshire, I was invited to join the board of directors of the Association of Business and Commerce, which was made up of most of the business interests in New Hampshire. The Association did some lobbying at the state government level and helped try to solve any statewide problems.

One of the problems in the southern part of the state was a shortage of Swiss screw machine operators. Several companies including Omni Spectra kept stealing each other's operators and wages were escalating out of control. As a member of the board at one of the board meetings, I advocated for the Association to do a needs survey wherein each company made some projections over the next five years in each category of workers. Then we could provide input to the local colleges and vo-tech schools for their training programs.

The membership liked the idea and indeed we did that statewide survey. Sure enough, the survey showed that while there were quite a few categories of similar interest, one of the biggest was for Swiss screw machine operators and set-up people.

I met with the presidents of the competing companies and we put together a training program at the local vo-tech school, where each of us donated a

Gov. John Sununu

machine and an instructor. After a year, our problem eased, and after two years, it went away.

After the second year on the board of directors, I was elected the president of the Association. As president, I had several jobs, one of which was to schedule a meeting with the governor as the legislature was advocating an increase in the business and profits tax. This tax increase would affect every company and business in the state, so I scheduled a meeting for several other company presidents and me with Governor John Sununu.

He had obtained a PhD in mechanical engineering from MIT and had taught engineering at Tufts University for almost 20 years. In addition to being very smart he was very tough. After three years as governor, he became chief of staff for President George H.W. Bush.

"While I understand your concern and agree with your position, there is no way this bill isn't going to pass," he said with his characteristic bluntness. I'm sorry, there is nothing I can do."

Hmm. Fortunately, I had a back-up plan that the other company presidents had agreed might work.

"Governor, we understand your position, and we would like to propose an alternative," I said. "If we could echo the Federal Research and Development Tax Credit, here at the state level, that would help us offset the increase in business and profit tax.

"We would be the first state in the nation to put that tax credit in place, and it could encourage other companies to enter the state. If we could get a tax credit for the incremental increase in R&D expenses, it could improve the growth rate of the existing industrial and increase profitability."

Elizabeth Dole, Secretary of Transportation

"That's a great idea, I like it" said Governor Sununu. "I think I can sell that." He did, and the state legislature approved both bills.

I met Sununu again, close up and personal, later in the year. The Association of Business and Commerce had an annual meeting where a state of the union speech was given by me and a VIP guest gave the keynote address. The governor was always invited. The annual meeting was a big deal with probably 500 people attending.

The guest speaker that year was Elizabeth Dole, Secretary of Transportation, and wife of Senator Bob Dole.

So, there I was, sitting on the dais with Secretary Dole on my right, and Governor Sununu on my left. I was very privileged and fortunate to be able to witness and to participate a little bit in our three-way conversation during dinner.

I did a lot of listening and very little talking and learned a lot. I had to wonder, however, how in hell this kid from Battle Creek, Michigan who had just barely made it out of high school, had come to be in this position. After the program started, I got up and gave a little short talk about our accomplishments during the year and then introduced Governor Sununu. He, in turn, got up and talked about the great state of New Hampshire. He also got to introduce Elizabeth Dole. As good a speaker as Sununu was, she got up and blew everybody away. A very elegant and graceful person, she was also extremely articulate.

* * *

One day out of the blue I got a call from Merc, my old friend from Hawaii and the West Coast. He needed a job because there had been a big layoff at Ford.

I did get him a job as we were always looking for workers. Merc and Diane, who was his long-term girlfriend and about 20 years younger, moved to New Hampshire, bought a house in Nashua and lived there for the rest of their lives. Merc died 10 years later from lung cancer, and Diane followed him less than a year later.

Someone once told me that when someone died, that as long as a friend or relative thought of them they were still alive. I often think about my deceased friends, relatives, and men I served with. I think of Merc often.

* * *

I had initially accepted the job as vice president and general manager of the Merrimack, New Hampshire plant which was the second largest facility. As the new president was located at the Tempe, Arizona, plant I was put in charge of all other operations on the East Coast and our plant in Reading, England.

Overall, the company was losing money and had exhausted its cash reserves so this public company was in deep trouble. The major problem was in the largest plant in Waltham, Massachusetts and this became my responsibility.

The division designed and manufactured high frequency connectors of many different models. It was fairly large with 600 employees and a $4.5-

million-dollar backlog of open orders, 80 percent of which were late!

I met with the VP and general manager and asked him what he thought was the problem. He stated that he needed more capacity. I said I would like to meet with the VP of manufacturing. As we toured the shops I saw rows and rows of screw machines, most of which had glowing red lights on their housing. Screw machines are old fashioned implements that can make precision metal parts. They were originally designed and built in Europe and were principally used to make parts for the watch industry. Waltham was the capital of US watchmaking.

"The red lights are an indicator that the machine is not running," the VP told me. "It's either being fixed because of a breakdown or is in setup."

The plant had a capacity problem, was out of inventory for its standard catalog parts, and distributors were screaming that they could not sell what they didn't have and were deserting Omni Spectra for our competition. So machines down for any reason was a major problem!

"How many of the lights were down because of breakdown?" I then asked the VP

"Only two or three out of the 150 machines," he said.

As 110 machines had red lights and three were being fixed, that left only 40 machines running and 107 machines in setup mode.

"Why there were so many machines in set-up?" I asked.

"I don't have enough set-up mechanics."

"Why don't you hire more?"

"They are hard to find and they cost too much."

"You mean to tell me that every setup guy in Waltham works for us?"

"No, they just cost too much."

"How much do they cost?"

"About $20-$30 dollars an hour."

Hmm, that s a lot of money in 1977. I retired to my temporary office in the Waltham plant and did a quick analysis. Given the profitability associated with each running machine, I did a quick analysis and determined that it didn't matter how much you had to pay for setup mechanics! I met with the VP of manufacturing and went through the analysis and told him to hire as many setup mechanics as he needed to keep the machines running.

Was there anything else I could help him with? He said that if I could get the sales department to stop taking special orders he would not have to hire as many setup mechanics. I said I would look into it. I then met with the VP of sales and after looking at the late backlog asked him why he was taking so many orders for specials.

He replied that his boss had given him a mandate to grow the business by 20 percent and that was the only way he could do it. His boss was the VP and general manager of the plant. I had long ago come to the conclusion that a small profitable company was worth a lot more than a large unprofitable company so I said I would look into it.

I fired the VP and general manager. I then met with the VP of sales and general staff.

"Effective immediately, I am the new general manager," I told them. "We as the management of this division need to turn it around or the company is doomed!"

I then met privately with the VP of sales and told him there was no longer a 20 percent growth mandate and that he should stop taking orders for any more specials. He was to go through the late backlog and determine which customers were critical to our long-term growth and prioritize their orders. Further, that he should contact all of the customers who had ordered three of this and four of that and get them to cancel their order. Also, that if my orders didn't work, that I would take away his company car, and if that didn't work, I was going to hang him—and not by the neck!

The next problem was that we needed cash to support the hiring of more setup mechanics and purchase a few more screw machine to replace the old tired machines that were always in setup or repair.

I thought about it a little bit, then brought some of that West Coast craziness to the puzzle. I announced at my weekly staff meeting that we were all going to meet in the obsolete inventory warehouse after normal working hours at 5 p.m.

"Bring some old clothes to work," I told them. Gold was selling for over $2,200 an ounce and some of our products were gold-plated because gold was a superior conductor of high frequencies. As the inventory was considered obsolete, I felt that we could strip and reclaim the gold. We met every day and at the end of the week we had raised more than $100,000. A small start but a good one in that the management team started to understand that there were actions that we could take instead of sitting around waiting for the ax to fall.

Now that we had some money, we needed to buy some Swiss screw machines to replace and upgrade our old and broken machines in the Waltham plant.

I took the VP of manufacturing, Dominic Nania with me on a European trip. Our plan was to visit Switzerland, Germany, and France, finishing up in England before we flew home. It was a tough trip;

besides the time differential that we had to a customize our bodies to, we had the language differences, culture differences, and the pressure of going to four countries in six days.

It was worth it, however, as we ended up purchasing a dozen machines. That was the first time I had been able to spend some social time with Dominic, and one always learns a lot by traveling with someone. Time and time again over the next 10 years Dominic would prove his resourcefulness. He turned out to be one of my favorite people and I was highly distressed when I heard he had passed away a few years ago.

We received the machines, Dominic got them installed, and the division became profitable within four months! I hired a new general manager and resumed my broader duties. Six months later the company was marginally profitable. The Arizona division was still losing a lot of money so the board of directors decided to sell the company to M/A-Com the largest company in our industry.

HIGH-FLYER

During M/A-Com's due diligence I was asked to meet with their president and CEO for dinner. He was the youngest man to ever graduate from MIT with a PhD in physics at age 21. Dr. Lawrence Gould was also rumored to be very tough.

Anyway, we met for dinner and after the small talk (which didn't take very long with him), Dr. Gould said that the purpose of the dinner was for him to meet one of the officers of Omni Spectra to whom he was going to offer an employment contract as part of the acquisition.

I said I was surprised by that because I didn't want a contract. Larry replied that the Omni Spectra president from Arizona had said it was a deal killer if M/A Com didn't include employment contracts for the senior officers.

I replied that I would not accept an employment contract.

"I don't believe in contracts; if I'm given a job to do I expect to be rewarded commensurate with the achievement," I explained. "If I failed, the company should not be penalized for my failure,"

After M/A Com did the acquisition, I was immediately made president of all of Omni Spectra, and I never had a problem with Dr. Larry Gould.

M/A-Com had a very close relationship with MIT. Bill Pounds was on leave from his previous position as dean of the Sloan School (MIT's business school) and was now the personal advisor to the Rockefeller family and their foundation. He was also chairman of the board of directors of M/A-Com. The company had also set up a major program of master's degree level training program for all of their senior managers. I went through that program.

While I had been president of Omni-Spectra immediately after the acquisition I had hired Harlon Meal and Gabriel Brittan, both senior professors at the Sloan School, to help develop a machine loading and scheduling system to help optimize the performance of the Omni Waltham plant. I had also put the bid out to Harvard.

MIT won and they bragged it was because they were smarter and wrote a better proposal. I told them that it was not true, they got the job because they were cheaper! We kidded each other about that for a long time.

Over the next 13 years I rose through the ranks to the position of Chief Operating Officer for all of M/A-Com and was made a member of the board of directors. I was number two in the company. At that time, we had around 8,000 employees and 23 operating plants around the world as well as two joint ventures in Japan.

During my 13 years there Dr. Gould was fired. Then his COO, Dick Dibona, took over as CEO, had a stroke, and was replaced by Dr. Frank Brand, who was a nice guy but not equipped and didn't really want to be number one. He was replaced by the CFO Tom Burke. Tom was not an operating guy, had come up through the financial ranks and was not technical. There was a long-term employee, an MIT graduate who was the favorite to become the new chief operating officer. I was the new guy. Tom divided the company into two divisions. He gave half to Harry Wells, and half to me. He then said he would make a decision on a COO at the end of a year.

One of the units that was assigned to my group was the advanced semiconductor division. This group of scientists were tasked with bringing to market a set of products based on a new compound of materials called Gallium Arsenide, which had the properties of being able to conduct electricity much faster than silicon-based compounds. The problem was that they were losing a million dollars each month.

My knowledge of semiconductor chemistry and quantum physics was skimpy at best, so I had to get educated quickly if I was going to be able to stem the negative cash flow and earnings. I called the manager of the division who was also the chief scientist.

"I need your help learning something about your operation," I told him. "How about you coming by my office each night around 5:30 and teach me a little bit about Gallium Arsenide and what you think your problems are?"

"Sure, when do you want to start?" he said.

"How about tonight?"

Carmon proceeded to tutor me for about two weeks on the technical aspects of his product development. Then we started to discuss what he thought his problem was.

"Dick, we need to get to a quarter-micron geometry between the gate and the emitter."

"That sounds pretty small, what are you doing to get there?" I asked.

"We are running experiments on the mask and the exposure time."

"How close are you and how many experiments are you running per month?"

"I think we can get there with another four or five experiments, and we can run an experiment every two months," Carmon replied,

"Hmm. That means that you're talking eight to ten months more at a million per month," I said.

Suddenly, the problem wasn't a quarter micron problem, it was how do we speed up the experiment process. I had been through a process problem like this before.

"Carmon, go to your favorite butcher shop and buy two rolls of that brown butcher paper and take them into the conference room."

"Dick, we've got the highest tech operation in the company here and you're going to solve my problem with butcher paper?"

I laughed. "No, we're going to flow-chart the experiment process and see if we can think out of the box and speed up the process. Alert your scientists."

We did such a review and were able to shorten the process by over 50 percent. Three months later we had produced a quarter-micron gate-to-emitter configuration and we reduced the monthly loss to $100,000. A few months later the division launched their high-performance product line using their newly-acquired quarter-micron technology and as their revenues grew, they became profitable. All because of butcher paper.

At the end of the year Harry retired and I was appointed COO.

When Tom Burke became CEO we had a bunch of problems. One was a depressed stock price due to a weak balance sheet and performance in the "just barely" category. We needed cash so as the new COO, I huddled with the CFO (Chief Financial Officer) and we put together a cash management system. We stretched our payables, got aggressive on our accounts receivable, and set tough but doable inventory turnover targets for all of the 23 operating divisions. In six months, we had improved our cash position by $50,000,000. That generated an unintended consequences type of problem.

M/A-Com was recognized as the technology leader in our industry, the market leader in most of our product segments so we were an attractive company. I pointed out to Tom, who had come up through the financial ranks instead of the technology or marketing ranks, that with now well over $50 million in cash in the bank and a depressed stock price, some would say that we were now a healthy hostile takeover target.

Our options were to sell the company, make an acquisition, or do a stock buyback. I had no experience in the sophistications and subtleties of a stock buyback program and quite frankly, I was anxious to get back to improving the operations of several of the marginal divisions. Tom said he understood but wanted to think about it for a few days.

About a week or so later, Tom called me into his office.

"I have made some calls and have an alternative option and want to see if you are up for it?"

"Up for what?

"I think that with your help, I could raise the money to take the company private and increase your and my ownership by 10 times!"

"Wow, that sounds attractive, but what will the board of directors think about that? Wouldn't they be out of a job?"

"Yes they would," Tom said, "but we could give them an outgoing bonus, and they could exercise their stock options so they would be fine."

"Well, you know them better than I do, I'm a newcomer," I replied.

"What do we do? By my way of thinking, the stock price is currently around $15 and we have a market cap of a little over $325 million, and assuming we would have to offer a 10-20 percent premium, that means we would have to raise somewhere around $400 million to buy the company."

"Do you know who has that kind of money and does these kinds of deals because I sure don't." I said.

“I do, the trick is you have to convince them as chief operating officer that we can improve the operating performance of the company such that we can service the debt.”

“Okay,” I said. “Depending on the cost of that capital, I think we could do it. Our compliance costs of just being a public company are around two percent of revenue so we would save those costs just to start. What’s next?”

“You and I have to go to New York and make a presentation to the higher ups,” Tom said. “I’ve scheduled a meeting for next week Thursday. They’ll pick us up at the airport; we will have to fly commercial and not use the company planes.”

To make a long story short, there was a series of meetings over the next four weeks and Tom negotiated a deal where they would put up the money, make the public tender offer. and handle all of the legal and stock work. We were now at the point where we had to inform the M/A-Com board of directors what we had been doing.

Secrecy was absolutely critical throughout this entire process. If word of it got out the stock price would go up and could kill the deal.

Tom and I went into the board room. Tom, who was a member of the board, announced that we were prepared to resign our positions, had an offer lined up to purchase the company, and needed a decision. That's akin to throwing your company car keys on the table, not for the weak of heart. Thoreau said, "Men live lives of quiet desperation." This was one of those times.

The board members listened, then asked us to wait outside while they conferred. Those were the longest hours of my life since I waited for my son and daughter to be born! Two hours later the board asked us back in the room.

"We understand your position and offer, and recognize the precariousness of the company's situation, but we feel the best option is for the company to use its cash and our stock to acquire another company," said Bill Pounds, the chairman of the board.

"We know that Adams Russell has been nosing around and we think we could pick them up for around $100 million. We will not accept your resignations and would like both of you to remain in your present positions. Further, we would like to offer Mr. Hale a position on the board."

Tom accepted the board's position, and then so did I. That was my sole experience with Wall Street banks and hostile takeovers. That was enough; I had enough stress and drama in my life!

* * *

Three weeks later I was in St. Martin on vacation. I had not taken any time off for almost three years and was looking forward to sunny beaches and lots of Makers Mark! Suddenly the phone rang. It was Bill Pounds.

"Dick, I'm afraid I have some bad news. Tom Burke was killed this morning in an automobile accident on 495 while coming to work. I have called for an emergency board meeting for tomorrow and we would like you back here in Burlington.

"I checked on the jets and one of them is in California, and the other one is undergoing a major maintenance plan. The King Air is also down so we have chartered a private jet to pick you and your wife up in about four hours. Is that okay?"

"Jesus, Bill, of course it's okay, I will be ready. Has anybody been in contact with Tom's wife?"

Bill said yes.

"Incidentally, the news is picking this up now and they will probably try to get in contact with you," Bill added. "The stock market hasn't opened yet, but I expect the stock will get hit a bit. If the news people contact you, the proper response is, no comment. We'll put out a statement right after the board meeting."

We had the board meeting and I was asked to give an overview on the status of the company. I was then excused from the meeting—again! An hour later I rejoined the meeting.

"The company needs you in your operating role, as you don't have a replacement, and this is a two-man job," said the spokesman. "Bill knows Tom Vanderslice from here in Boston who is looking for a short-term job before he retires, but we would like you to be on the interview committee. You and several other board members will do the interview. Tom is highly overqualified but interested because it is close to his home here on Beacon Hill."

Tom Vanderslice

Great, I have gone from prime candidate to a position where I get to interview my boss! Tom told me later in private that I was the only interviewee that talked about what I felt the company needed, the others all talked about compensation.

Tom had come up through the ranks at GE but left there and became president of GT&E, a huge public company many times larger than M/A-Com. Tom was nearing retirement age and was seen as an interim CEO. He had homes on Beacon Hill in Boston, Cape Cod, and Naples Florida. Tom was a PhD. in engineering with 40 years of experience.

I became Tom's number two. I was still living in New Hampshire and commuting into Burlington, Massachusetts some 50 miles and an hour away. Tom ordered me to start taking a limo to work as he did from Boston, some 10 miles away from the corporate headquarters. He was a big company guy.

I said that I could not take a limo to the company. I would lose the respect of all of the managers and employees and I needed to spend a lot of my time with them in the plants. He grudgingly said okay but it did point out a difference in philosophies that would ultimately cause some problems.

* * *

Tom Vanderslice called me into his office right after he reported on board as the new president and chief executive officer. I reported as requested as it was my job as second in command to carry out the policies that he developed for the company.

"Good morning boss, what's on your mind?"

Tom smiled. "Dick, I noticed when I did a little due-diligence before I took the job here, that there are 'Reserved Parking' signs in front of most of the local plants. Did you call for those signs and are they at all 23 plants?"

"No, I didn't," I said. "They were here when I joined the company, I would guess they have been there for a long time. Why do you ask?"

"I would like you to eliminate all reserved parking at all of our plants, effective immediately—okay?"

"Yes sir, I'll take care of it," I said, but my mind started racing. Given the issues we have with the San Diego division, our need to expand the Waltham plant, and the status of the joint venture in Japan which appears to be going sideways, why was this so important? My skepticism must have been written all over my face.

"Dick, it's important," Tom said.

"Okay," I replied, "you're the boss, I'll take care of it." I still didn't get it. This would be our first official policy change and he is concerned about reserved parking? This by the CEO of the company who has a chauffeur-driven limo take him 10 miles from Beacon Hill in Boston to corporate here in Burlington? This should be interesting.

I went back to my office and drafted a memo to all 23 plant managers asking them to immediately remove all 'reserved parking' spaces and signs at their plants.

A week later during our morning briefing, Tom said, "Dick I see that you have eliminated most of the reserved parking spaces and signs, but there are still two plants that have them up. What's the problem?"

"I'm not sure what the problem is but I'll take care of it," I said, "but to tell you the truth, boss, I'm still confused about why this is so important."

Tom smiled again. He didn't do that very often so I guess I was lucky twice so far.

"Dick, I don't care one tinker's dam about reserved parking, I'm interested in the response time of the corporation to a simple policy change," he said. "If our response time is faster than the competition then we will learn faster than the competition and we will win."

Wow! That's why he is the Ph.D. and CEO, and I am in second place!

* * *

I was scheduled to attend several sales meetings in Europe as part of my responsibilities as chief operating officer of MA/Com. My daughter, Laura, had just graduated from college so I decided that I would take her on my trip as an informal graduation present.

I was scheduled for meetings in Paris, Rome, and in Brussels, Belgium, which was where Erik Vevey lived. Erik was head of all international sales, spoke French, German, Italian, and English and was an old friend known to me even before I had joined MA/Com. Erik decided that because my daughter was with me, he was going to host a special dinner before we left to fly back home.

The top restaurant in all of Europe happened to be in Brussels. Erik knew the owner well and got us a reservation for six people the night before we were to leave.

As we walked into the restaurant, the owner met us and asked us if we preferred to eat in or out?

I replied, "Out."

The owner then pushed a button and the entire roof of the executive dining room opened up to reveal the stars and moon above! We then were seated at the table in the middle of the wood-paneled room. The owner announced that in our honor, he was going to serve us the same meal that had earned him the Five-Key award as the best restaurant in Europe.

Six male waiters in black tie stood discreetly behind each of us and attended to our every need. Water glasses were filled if you took even a sip, dishes were cleared as we finished, as this was a multicourse dinner; wine glasses were filled immediately as a different wine was served with each course.

When a serving was announced, all of the waiters paraded in the room and then took positions next to all six of us. Upon a silent signal they each placed the silver tureen in front of us.

"Viola," they exclaimed in unison and lifted the covers of the tureens. When the dinner was completed, the owner entered the room again, as he was always checking on us.

"How did you like the dinner, Mr. Hale?"

"I have never had such a meal, your wine selections were perfect for each course, and I cannot thank you enough for granting my daughter and me such an exquisite experience." I meant every word. Then I asked, "I am curious however, and I apologize for being too forward, but just how many bottles of wine do you keep here in your restaurant?"

He smiled. "Would you like to see the wine cellar?"

"I would be honored."

So, he ushered me into the cellar of the restaurant where there were floor-to-ceiling rows and rows of bottled wines.

"Generally we keep around 18,000 bottles here, but of course we have two other cellars, one in Paris, and one in Rome," said the manager. "I have a full-time sommelier that travels all over the world, just buying wines for me."

It was quite a night, quite a dinner and a shared experience that I am sure neither of us will forget. And I got to share it with my daughter. I am a lucky guy!

* * *

Whenever I ever took a family member on a trip, I always paid for their share of the expenses. I only violated that self-imposed rule one time. When my parents were still alive, I had invited them to spend Christmas with me and the family in New Hampshire. Dad said that they couldn't afford the air fare, and when I said that I would pay for it, he told me I couldn't do that.

This was a very proud man that would arm-wrestle you to see who would pay for the coffee, so I knew that wasn't going to work.

I looked into another option and saw that one of the corporate jets was scheduled to return from California just before Christmas to the corporate headquarters in Boston. I made some arrangements with our scheduler, then called Dad.

"Dad, the corporate plane is coming back from California on the 19th and could stop in Battle Creek and pick you and mom up and bring you here to New Hampshire," I told him. "It's right on their way, would that be okay?"

"That sounds okay, it's one of your planes?"

"Yes, Dad, I know the pilots, they will take good care of you."

"Okay."

Anyway, the Learjet stopped in Battle Creek, picked up my parents, and dropped them off in New

Hampshire and we had a great Christmas. Later I asked one of the pilots how it went.

"Your dad tucked your mom into one of the seats in the back and then came into the cockpit where he stayed the rest of the trip. He told us some stories of his old barnstorming days in that Swallow! He's quite a guy."

Yes, he is!

* * *

Several months later Tom called a board meeting in Boca Raton and wives were invited. So, we all flew down to Boca in the corporate jets and stayed there for three days. There were shopping trips for the ladies, deep sea fishing for the men, and fine dining every night.

We had a two-hour board meeting at a private club on the third day. As the chief operating officer, I knew that waiting on my desk back in Burlington was a list of 500 employees that I had to lay off because of the reduction in the defense budget. This was the other side of the peace dividend after the US won the Cold War.

I got back to Burlington and executed the layoff because it was my job. One of the employees affected went home, told his wife that he had just lost his job, got into his truck, drove out into the woods of New Hampshire, and killed himself.

A few days later I resigned. I walked away from a $400,000 a year job. I had had enough! If this was the conduct for large public companies, I didn't need it. I was just a kid from Michigan and this didn't fit in with my set of values. It was 1993.

I never regretted leaving M/A-Com. One thing I had learned at this stage of my business career was that the real benefit of having a little money wasn't being able to buy things. Having a little money afforded you the freedom to do the right thing and still take care of your family. I remember a comment from Paul Tsongas, former senator from Massachusetts and candidate for president of the United States. Paul was a member of our board of directors. One day I asked him how he defined character.

Sen. Paul Tsongas

"Doing the right thing even when it hurts." Paul was a stand-up guy and was one of my heroes. I have to wonder if I would have had the courage to do the right thing if I had not had enough money to ensure that I could take care of my family.

Granted, there would be a step down in lifestyle, no more corporate jets, less spending money, but there would still be enough to meet our financial commitments and responsibilities.

I guess that at some point in your life you have to recognize and honor what's really important to you. I had always been able to draw a line in the sand and say, "Push me into a corner, cross that line, and I will fight back."

I was now 56 years old, still full of energy, and unemployed. Although I had received several offers from corporate America I had come to dislike the politics of large corporations.

I preferred the environment of smaller non-public companies where performance alone determined if you would survive. I understood and liked that way of working.

BACK TO EARTH

I was asked to join the board of directors of another public company, Parlex, which I accepted. I served on that board for 10 years until the company was sold. I much enjoyed being a member of Parlex's board as it was a non-political group of senior experienced executives.

I also did some free consulting for a company called Watson Technology. Jack Watson was a retired systems engineer from Raytheon that I had met socially and he had asked me to look at his company. He sensed that he was in trouble with his investor. His investor was Michael Chang, a second-generation Harvard-educated manager of Chang Capital. Chang Capital was a family owned company with over $3 billion invested.

Jack had come up with an idea for a TV system that was based on the principal that you paid for only what you watched. The system concept relied on a super sensitive receiver that could detect from outside the home what channel you were watching.

Jack had surrounded himself with several vice presidents that were smooth talkers but were not technologists. They pretended to know about business but spent their time thinking about which corporate jet they were going to purchase.

Watson Technology had gone through $10 million of Chang's money over the three years of their existence and had not even built a prototype receiver. Now Jack was almost out of money.

I spent time with Jack and outlined what had to be done. He asked me if I would accompany him to a meeting scheduled with Michael Chang and present the plan. I said I would and ended up meeting with Chang and some of his advisors.

Jack was asking for another $2 million. I made the presentation.

"I will give you the $2 million for another 10 percent of the company with the stipulation that Mr. Hale run the company," Michael said. Jack then asked me to become president and help him out

I said I would, but with two conditions: one was that I had absolute control as I was going to fire some of his friends; second, I would only commit for one year. Jack and Michael agreed and I was starting a new adventure.

In a private conversation with Michael, I asked him what he was worried about. With $3 billion invested, he was making almost a million dollars a day. Michael's answer surprised me. Michael said he was worried whether or not he had provided protection down far enough in his family because kidnapping was always a threat if you had that level of money. He said that it happened all the time, but you would never hear about it because it was always settled privately. Not something I would have to worry about!

I promptly fired three of Jack's four VPs as I needed the money to hire some engineers. The receiver which was the heart of the entire system was going to require a sensitivity that had never been achieved before. To make a long story short, one year later I called a meeting with members of the Chang company in attendance and said that I had good news and bad news.

The good news was that in the lab is a receiver that works, just barely, but it does work. The bad news is that if X is what we can sell the system for, the best-case cost of the system is 4X. Therefore, I recommended that we shut down the company and return the remaining $1 million to the Chang Company and sell the patent and other intellectual property. It was the right thing to do, but again difficult, especially for Jack. This we did and I was unemployed again!

* * *

Because I was deeply involved in the sailing world, I ran into a guy named Dodge Morgan. Dodge was famous for inventing the first car-mounted radar detector, "Whistler," and had become a very wealthy man. He was a great guy to drink with and had lots of stories.

I did a sailing trip with Dodge and two other guys to Bermuda, five days sailing from Portland Maine to St Georges in Bermuda shedding clothes all the way as we left Maine in November and it was snowing.

Dodge had used some of his wealth to build a custom sailboat which he used to become the first American to sail nonstop around the world by himself. He had also invested in a small company located on the Maine—New Hampshire state line which made electronic telephone headsets. When I told him the Watson Technology story he said, "At least you did the right thing. Do you want a job?"

"Tell me about it," I said as I motioned for another drink.

He described the company and asked if I thought I could get it profitable enough to sell.

I then made a mistake and said yes, relying on Dodge's comments without doing any due-diligence.

On the first day that I reported for duty as the new president the phone rang. I picked up the phone and found out that I was talking to the head of the "work-out division" of the local bank who informed me that we had 90 days to get into debt conformance or the bank was going to foreclose.

Wow! Stupid! Testimony to the fact that you should never let down your guard and that you should always exercise those cautionary actions that had made you successful so far. My first day on the job. Hmm.

I negotiated a payment schedule that we could afford and laid off a bunch of employees that were relatives of the former president and VP of sales. The company was doing about five million in sales per year and losing money. The company was selling into a large market dominated by two large companies. VXI was also selling exclusively through a set of distributors that were also selling the headsets from the major competitors who were five to ten times the size of VXI. No wonder the company had stumbled!

That selling channel was owned by the competitors and they would never let you out of the corner. I needed a strategy, because just cleaning up the operations would not get us where we had to go to make the company saleable.

* * *

There was a company in existence then called Dragon Systems. Dragon's engineering team had come up with a software package that allowed for speech to text, and text to speech that was in the 90 percent accuracy range. That meant that for every 100 words, 10 could be wrong and then had to be corrected which slowed down the process and was an impediment to sales.

It turns out that there were two barriers to getting the accuracy rate above 90% and VXI could help solve one of them. They were starting to market the speech recognition software under the tradename "Naturally Speaking." Even with the accuracy problems, they were approaching sale of a million units.

They were selling a cheap, noisy headset from China with each software suite. We bought several packages and did a lot of testing with our headsets. We then designed and built headsets with noise-cancelling technology. That eliminated a lot of background noise and had a dramatic improvement on the accuracy metric as the computer did not have to work as hard to eliminate noise.

We did a Coke-Pepsi test for the senior people at Dragon and subsequently sold them over four million headsets over the next few years. We called the headset "The Parrot."

The Chinese then copied what we were doing and cut the price in half so that we couldn't compete as Dragon reluctantly switched vendors.

VXI had a good engineering department and I had learned something from a book called "Only the Paranoid Survive" by Andy Grove, president of Intel. He saw that Intel was losing the memory chip market, also to the Chinese. Buried deep in the bowels of Intel was a small group of engineers who were working on a new type of chip, something called a micro-processer. Andy Grove empowered the small group of inventors, and quickly Intel became the market leader in micro-processer chips. With a much more complex and difficult to copy unit, Intel became the company we know today.

We at VXI had been working on developing a wireless headset using the Bluetooth protocol. We combined our new Bluetooth wireless headset with our previous noise cancelling headset technology and called it the "Blue Parrot" which became semi-famous. We sold the Blue Parrot into the speech recognition market at premium prices and made a lot of money. That lasted for quite a while before the Chinese countered as they always do.

In the large volume retail markets, you have about 18 to 24 months before they respond, so you better get your investment payback in that timeframe.

In the meantime, our "Call Center" basic headset market remained under stress and was starting to lose money. This was the first product of the company and as such was very close to Dodge Morgan's heart. He felt that if we just put on more distributors, we could win the battle. I disagreed, stating that I was trying to build the technology leader that kept us always on the front edge of emerging markets and that the right strategy was to build a company with salable value. He disagreed, and the arguments grew in frequency and intensity. Dodge had been very successful in his mind, had very strong opinions and could never be wrong.

I continued with my strategy. As an example, we had accidently heard that long-haul truck drivers were frustrated with their cell phone method of communicating because they had to hold the cell phone while they drove. I sent our marketing people to truck stops to find out how widespread the frustration was as well as how much would they pay for a solution. Did the solution also need to be wireless?

We ended up developing a marketing and sales packaging for the trucking industry using our noise-cancelling wireless speech recognition headset with an improved antenna to give us more range.

We sold $1.8 million dollars' worth in the first 12 months. We sold the product through two distributors who didn't have anything to offer in that space but whose product line was pointed at the truck stops and trucker market.

Despite this, Dodge and I continued to disagree so I said the hell with it and resigned. Dodge had developed cancer a year before. A year or so after I resigned, he passed away. It was 2010. His kids sold VXI for $35 million dollars right after Dodge passed away. So VXI had gone from being unsaleable and imbedded in a work-out group to being worth $35 million. Admittedly, it had taken 10 years.

While we disagreed on a fair number of things, we hung out together a lot, as we were both single, drank too much, and also had a lot of fun together. He was a colorful guy with a lot of adventures and accomplishments, and he passed too soon. When I was given the "Sailor of the Year" award by the Maine Ocean Racing Sailing Association, Dodge had been one of the key speakers. My 47-foot *Bandito* had never lost a race to his 60-foot *American Promise*.

* * *

When I left VXI and the company was later sold, my senior staff kept in touch with me. I'd meet one or two of them for lunch or dinner once every month or so. We had worked well together and there was a lot of mutual respect.

Anyway, during one of the dinners, someone said, "Why don't we start a company?" A lot of discussion ensued with me staying quiet. Everyone was excited. Then someone asked me if I was willing to be involved and would I agree to be president.

I wasn't sure I was up for doing another startup but said I would think about it. After a week or so, I contacted everybody and said that I would agree to get involved if they were all committed. We knew quite a bit about manufacturing and marketing headsets after 10 years but had no wish to dive back into any of the VXI worlds. We were driven to start a company because we all liked and respected each other and enjoyed working together, not because we had a vision.

We started meeting almost weekly to talk about our new company. A convenient place for our meetings was the Wentworth Hotel, a place in New Hampshire where there was a good bar and a so-so restaurant.

I have always followed the idea that if you uncover a problem, you have also uncovered an opportunity. As all of us had frequented McDonalds and other drive-through restaurants, we were aware of the sound problems associated with ordering our food. Further investigation revealed that the most critical detriment to restaurant revenue was slow times through the drive-through due to bad communications.

I went out to a bookstore and bought six copies of a book called "Fast Food Nation," written in 2005, which gave a lot of information on the industry which had now changed the name of the segment of the industry to the "QSR market" (Quick Reaction Market). It was required reading for our next meeting.

We thought that with our noise cancelling, wireless headset experience at VXI, we could bring a new level of capability to the industry. The existing communication systems in the QSR industry were headset systems that talked to a base station where the system volume and clarity were adjusted. The problem was that the base station was so complicated and difficult to use that nobody bothered to adjust the system. The industry-wide sound systems were serviced by two long-term residents of the industry, a company in California, HME, and a small company headquartered in Minnesota called 3M!

HME and 3M were selling systems that had not been updated for many years and we figured that HME would be the fastest to respond, which would take them about a year. 3M would be longer due to their vast bureaucracy.

Our challenges then were to raise some capital, design a system, and figure out the best way to sell and market our system. We figured that would take us a year to get to market. In the meantime, we had to do our work staying in the weeds as much as we could. It was my job to raise the capital.

After 50 years of raising various amounts of capital, \$100,000 to \$450 million, from a variety of sources, such as angels, banks, VCs, large investment bankers and financial and strategic investors, I've concluded that the best chance for success has been by putting myself in the seat of the investor and answering six questions.

1. Is it real? Is there a real problem that needs fixing or is this a typical story where an engineer says "I can do this and it is so neat" - but nobody will buy it because it does not solve a real problem or demonstrate a better way to do something and thus save money and/or time?

2. Can I win? What is the competitive environment? Does the competition control the selling channels? Can they "out muscle" me due to their size? How aggressive is the competition? Are they old, big, and slow, or are they fast and aggressive with resources?

3. Is it worth it? Is this opportunity one that will allow me to get a return that meets my needs? Does the risk/reward level feel comfortable?

4. What is the market risk? – Is the market slow to react, is it receptive to new ideas and suppliers, is it growing or declining? How big is it and does this opportunity require a unreasonable or reasonable market share position? (Pimm's Study)

5. What is the technical risk—are these guys going to have to reinvent the laws of physics? What is the probability that the competition has something better in their engineering lab? What is the history of the market? Does the market embrace new ideas and new ways of doing things?

6. What is the operational risk? Does this team have the management strength to "get it done?" or are they weak in certain areas? What is their history? Is there a team?

The difficult part is to assess the audience as to their level of capacity, interest, and which questions are they most worried about? After making such an assessment I then try to put together a presentation that answers those questions.

The website, selling literature, advertising, and investment presentation would all be well served by consistent answers to the six questions listed above.

I was able to raise $10 million over the first few months for our start-up. We named the company

"Wentworth Technology," found a home, and started work. A year later we had a wireless headset system that used the first active and passive noise cancelling technology and a base station patterned after Steve Job's touch-phone technology.

We tested our headset and base station products by submitting them to "the grandmother test." If a grandmother couldn't operate the system, then it was too complicated and not intuitive enough. We started selling systems at $3,000 to $7,000 each depending on how many headsets the customer ordered. Again, stealing from Apple's playbook, we gave several systems to Dunkin Donuts and Burger King to get some attention. This marketing strategy worked quite well and these companies became our largest customers. Over a period of the next five years, we sold systems to every QSR chain in the business, except McDonalds. We never penetrated the largest QSR restaurant in the world.

After about a year, I got a call from a VP of 3M. He wondered if I might be interested in talking about a possible business alliance. I said sure, it never hurts to talk.

Two VPs from 3M showed up at our doorstep in southern Maine a week later and then I made a mistake. They obviously were interested in acquiring Wentworth, and I said no. We were whipping their butt as they had the weakest system which was failing in the field and were in second place to HME. I was interested in their selling channel which was distributor-centric compared to HME, who sold direct through their own employee-based sales force, which we could not afford.

We were unable to agree on terms and their response time was terrible. In a competitive market, if your competition's response time is quicker than yours it means their learning is faster than yours, and eventually, you are going to lose. We were much smaller, and much faster at every aspect of our business than 3M and were beating them anyway so why give up so soon? We had only been in business for about three years.

"Dick, we may have a problem," our VP of engineering said one day. "Imbedded in both the headsets and the base stations are a chipset that comes to us from Germany and I was just informed that they are going to stop manufacturing the chip in about six months."

"How about another manufacturer?"

"There aren't any others."

"Can we redesign around it using a chipset that has more than one manufacturer?"

"It's possible, but those chipsets were perfect for our configuration and even if I can find an alternative, it would take at least 9 months to a year. Those chips are at the heart of the system design."

"How about buying up any inventory at their factory and in their selling channel? That might buy us some time."

"I think we can do that, but we better hurry because everybody using that chipset will be facing the same problem."

"Do it—I'll find the money."

We were able to acquire enough chips to last us about nine months. Dave was right, we had a problem!

Problems generally come in pairs, and this chip problem was the mother of all problems, because it ultimately led to a total restructuring of the company, including a name change. There are two kinds of capital: equity capital means ownership of a portion of the business; debt capital is a loan. One of our investors was in the debt category, and they further insisted that a life insurance policy for $250,00 be put on my life with them as the beneficiary and the premiums paid by the company.

This problem was causing us to go through so much cash that we were in trouble. We made it through the year, but now we had to negotiate a deal with the debt holder who was acting very tough. We owed them a little over $280,000. They wanted to foreclose but I pointed out that we could not manufacture or sell any more headset systems, because there were no more chips. I had stopped taking a salary when the problem surfaced as I knew we were going to run out of money and I would not be able to raise any more capital given the situation.

I had an idea for a new product (eventually the idea resulted in a patent) and another of the original Wentworth gang and I made an offer to personally purchase the assets of Wentworth Technology. We would take on the debt at a reduced rate and do away with the life insurance policy which was costing $1,000 a month. I agreed also to not take a salary until the debt was paid off.

The idea was to use the new company which I named LD Electronics after my kids, Laura and David, to repair the Wentworth Systems that needed attention and use the proceeds to foster the patent legal work and underwrite the development of the new product.

That is exactly what we have done. All five of the original Wentworth founders are still involved at various levels of effort. We have a working prototype; the debt is down to under $100,000, and we have a patent on the technology. Chip selection has not as yet been made! Unfortunately, we are still paying the premiums on the life insurance policy. I have to admit it's a bit difficult working with an investor who's betting I'm going to die. I am committed to outliving the bastards!

A portrait of Bandito in action

SAILING

It was San Francisco Bay; the water was very cold and it was blowing like hell! The fleet was down to a very few boats and we had capsized twice already, as had every boat. Our two-man 17-foot-long 505 trapeze boat was upside down and one of the portholes into the starboard air tank had popped out and the tank was filled with water, so we couldn't get the boat right side up. Worse yet the fog was coming in through the Golden Gate. The water was very cold.

Bruce and I were in the water trying to get the boat back right side up to no avail. Pretty soon Bruce said he was having trouble holding on to the boat so I took one of the spinnaker lines and tied him to the boat. The fog was getting thicker and we couldn't see anything beyond 10 feet as we were upside down drifting toward Alcatraz Island.

I knew that the cold would get to me pretty soon, so I started to tie myself to the 17-foot boat thinking at least they would find the bodies. For a moment the fog parted near us and a 40-foot sailboat with his sails down and under power saw us and came about as they knew we were in serious trouble.

They hoisted us aboard their boat and got us down below out of the wind. They tied our boat to theirs and started to haul us and our upside down 505 to the St Francis Yacht Club. We arrived an hour later. At least something good came out of it all, as the SBRA (Small Boat Racing Association) mandated that effective immediately that all participants in their races had to wear wet-suits.

One of the 505 races that was held every other year and one that you had to qualify for was the "505 Marathon." The race started at the St. Francis Yacht Club just inside the Golden Gate bridge on the San Francisco side, went up to a buoy just inside the bridge, then finished at the dock at the Palo Alto Yacht Club, some 40 miles away.

To get there, you had to sail under the Bay bridge that went over to Treasure Island, then through a draw bridge about 10 miles from Palo Alto which had to be opened for us by the bridge keeper, then up the channel to the yacht club.

The deal with the bridge keeper was that when we got close, you blew your whistle, and he would open the bridge so we could sail through as our masts wouldn't clear the bridge otherwise. There were generally about 25-30 boats that qualified and there was a big party at the yacht club when everybody finished.

The 505 was only 17 feet long, but was very light and very, very, fast if sailed well. The record time was a little under three hours which meant you averaged over thirteen knots.

The year I qualified for the race, Dennis Surtees, the current US champion was leading at the drawbridge and we were probably around sixth or seventh. When Dennis approached the bridge and blew his whistle to notify the bridge-keeper we were coming, nothing happened. The fleet was closing in so Dennis and his crew, capsized his boat and swam the boat under the bridge followed by the first seven boats doing the same.

A few moments later, the bridge-keeper woke up and opened the bridge for the rest of the fleet. I think we ended up fourteenth! We ended up having a great party with many stories about the bridge, and a trophy dedicated for the next race called "First to the Bridge."

After 10 years of sailing in San Francisco Bay and New England waters, I entered the Lightning class of sailboats. There were a lot of Lightnings there and they were very competitive. I liked the boat as it was fast, could be trailered at 19 feet, and required a three-man crew, which allowed me a chance to race with my kids.

I remember one race where we were leading, it was fairly windy, we had the spinnaker up and had to jibe. My daughter and son were with me and Laura stood up on the foredeck to jibe the spinnaker pole – and promptly fell over the side.

We were in a lake in Maine with about 10-15 other boats. I remember my son yelling because he knew that to take the spinnaker down shorthanded, turn around, go back, and pick her up would cost us the race.

"Dad, do we have to go back and get her?" he asked.

I laughed. "Yes, you have to end the race with the same number you start with." So, we did, and I

Bandito, my 47-foot racing sailboat, crew of 10-12

think by the time we got it all sorted out we ended up 10th. David lit into his sister for quite a while.

Two weeks later, we were down on Cape Cod and it was a big fleet with the US champion racing. He was leading, we were in third place and had to tack. As we tacked, David missed the hiking straps and fell overboard. Wow, I didn't know my daughter even knew such words!

Ten years of sailing Lightnings in New England with my kids was a joy, but my body was starting to give out so I moved into larger keelboats, still racing, but now with a crew of 12 on the day races, and 10 on the overnight races.

While we did a lot of round the buoys races typically 15-20 miles, I remember a 225-mile overnight race from Portland, Maine to Yarmouth, Nova Scotia. We were fortunate to finish first. We had a rule that we never drank during a race. So after going across the finish line we were folding sails and cleaning up the boat as we motored into town. Now that the race was over we were drinking.

As we neared the town, the Royal Canadians came alongside. They were heavily armed so when they asked the crew who was in charge, the guys quickly pointed at me.

The officer inspected all of our passports and papers then asked me if we had any drugs on board.

"No, sir."

He then asked me if we had any weapons on board.

"No, sir," I replied.

He then asked me if we had any alcohol on board.

"Not anymore."

He paused, then chuckled and said, "Welcome to Nova Scotia and congratulations!"

Over the 25 years that I raced in New England we won the Class A Season Championship 12 times and once five years in a row, which had never been done before. I also sailed to Bermuda with three other men which is yet another story. I also did the Marblehead to Halifax race, did not do very well, but had a good time!

I sailed from Portland, Maine to Bermuda one November with three other sailors called "The Body Bag Crew." The reason for the name was that at 70 years old, I was the youngest of the crew. I was replacing a former member who didn't make it. These guys had been doing this trip for years and did carry a body bag on board the 50-foot sailboat.

They told me that as the newest and youngest member of the crew, I had to take a refresher course from the Red Cross on first aid. I took the course, and when questioned by the three guys as to what I had learned, I told them; "You guys are going to die."

They took me anyway. It was November in Maine and actually snowing as we stood out of the main channel in Portland and set sail. Five days later we pulled into St. George's harbor in Bermuda and moored alongside the customs dock. As soon as we cleared customs we headed for the beach and the nearest bar where I was introduced to a "Dark and Stormy", a cocktail of dubious distinction made up of ginger beer and rum. I found out two things that day. One, the Dark and Stormy was supposedly invented in Bermuda and two, these guys were older, but they sure knew how to drink!

I once sailed from Ft. Myers, Florida, to the Dry Tortugas, a collection of islands 75 miles west of Key West. It was an overnight trip and upon arriving we anchored off of the main island that housed Fort Jefferson. As we took the dingy onto the island, I noticed an old beat-up wooden rowboat pulled up on the sandy beach.

As the Dry Tortugas are part of the US and guarded by the park rangers, I asked the local ranger about the rowboat.

"That's quite a story. Six guys escaped from Cuba in that old boat," he said. "They ran out of gas about three miles out and swam the rest of the way. I didn't know what to do because it's never happened before, so I called my boss in Key West and he sent a boat that picked them up two days ago and took them to Key West for processing.

"They have reached US soil and are now in line to become US citizens. How those guys were able to navigate to the islands is a miracle. The islands are maybe two feet above sea level and with visibility from a rowboat limited by the curvature of the earth to a horizon five to six miles away, it's unbelievable. The closest point in Cuba is Havana, and that's got to be at least 100 miles from here."

I spent a lot of money over the years, had a great time, and met many great people. I had many boats over the years, one for 17 years. Sailboat racing is one of the better ways in the world to waste money!

Once a year a special event was held in and around the city of Portland, Maine where I lived and sailed. The event was known as the annual "MS Regatta." It raised money to combat MS and was a three-day event. The first day was a large auction and party held outdoors right on the waterfront. The second day was the central focus of the event, the actual sailboat regatta with more than 100 boats participating in several classes. The third day, Sunday, consisted of tugboat races held in the Portland Harbor. My boat, *Bandito,* was in class A with about 10-12 boats participating. The race for our class was generally about 20 miles long.

The morning of the regatta I received a call from one of my best friends, Merle Hallett. Merle was the creator of the Regatta weekend some 20 years earlier and was still the chief promoter. We raced against each other for most of those 20 years and were still good friends.

"Dick, I have a favor to ask," Merle said.

"What's the favor?"

"I have a family friend who has MS but she wants to go on the race. You have a big boat (same size as Merles) and I thought she would be safer on your boat." What Merle wasn't saying was that we were in the same class, and he wanted to beat my ass in the regatta! Merle was 10 years older, owned a boatyard, and was the defending champion for this race.

After asking if she could handle the rigors of a 45-foot sailboat in heavy wind as we tacked back and forth out of the Portland channel on our way out to the open sea, I agreed to take her.

She showed up on the dock where we were tied up. As I watched her being helped out of the handicapped van I thought "Oh, Oh, Merle got me again."

My 12-man crew looked at me and I just shrugged. Her name was Mary, and as we made the introductions and helped her onto the boat, I assigned Frank, whose racing position on the boat was always right behind me taking care of the running backstays as we tacked back and forth, to take care of her.

There was one other woman on board, another total novice and a girlfriend of one of my crew members. We normally didn't allow women on board when we were racing. I told Frank that his job during the race was to help Mary get from one side of the boat to the other as we heeled over from one tack to the other. I also assigned another crew member to do Frank's normal job with the backstays.

Anyway, we started the race, and it was quite windy. We had the number three jib up (the smallest jib we carried other than the storm jib) and the boat was heeling at about 25-30 degrees as we started out of the channel. I had to concentrate on steering so was not able to look behind me. I kept bumping into someone with an extra person behind me and forgetting who was there.

"Jesus, Frank you've got a big ass," I yelled above the wind. Then I realized it wasn't Frank, it was our guest.

US-32008
US-32008

Frank

In the meantime, my crewmember's girlfriend was screaming at him as we heeled in the strong wind.

"This wasn't in the brochure, you asshole," she wailed. "You're never gonna touch me again!"

A good time was had by all!

We won the race, and I gave the trophy to Mary and thanked Merle for giving me such a good crew. I rubbed it in by adding, "And if it hadn't been for Mary we probably wouldn't have won."

A week later, I got a letter in the mail from Mary, thanking me for "one of the greatest experiences of her life."

You just never know!

* * *

As I walked into the downtown Portland Maine restaurant to attend a luncheon meeting, I passed a table and Rob Baldacci said, "Hi Dick."

Sitting at Rob's table was a guy who looked vaguely familiar and a woman that I didn't know. Rob was a local lawyer and business leader whose brother was the governor of Maine. I responded, and Rob introduced his guests, F. Lee Bailey, the famous lawyer, and Debby Elliot, his companion. We exchanged the usual pleasantries, but I had to excuse myself as I was already late for my meeting.

I had met Rob a month or two earlier in the Boothbay Harbor Yacht Club where he had crewed on a boat that we had competed with during the regatta. Generally speaking, I had always tried to stay as far away from lawyers as I could, but Rob was a standup guy, and we got along well. Anyway, I was impressed that Rob knew such a famous personage but didn't dwell on the chance meeting.

About two weeks later, my phone rang, and it was F. Lee Bailey inviting me to his birthday party to be held at a house in Cumberland next to where I lived in Falmouth Maine. I was surprised and wondered why I was getting an invitation but accepted. What I didn't know was that Rob had been talking to Lee about me and my background as a sailor and a businessman.

Rob, as part of his many adventures, ran a business-focused TV show and had invited me to be a guest on his show scheduled in about a month.

I showed up at Lee's party where there were about 20 people including Rob, his wife, and Debby Elliot. Lee and I talked and he indicated that he loved Maine and had spent many summers here as a kid growing up. He was currently planning to move from the Boston area into Maine and was applying to the state for his law license so that he could resume his law practice. He then asked me if I would be willing to testify on his behalf as a character witness.

F. Lee Bailey

"I have only testified three times before, once in a patent-trade secret case, and twice in divorces, and I lost all three cases so I might not be the best witness," I told him.

He laughed and said, "Peter DeTroy, (the head of a large well-respected Portland law firm) will be contacting you."

The next week, Peter called me and we arranged a meeting where he could give me some guidance as to what to expect. I was testifying in front of the governing board of the Maine Bar Association.

Peter said that before the hearing, I needed to review the trial history of a trial and subsequent appeal of a trial held in Florida where Lee had been disbarred.

Wow! How could it be that this famous lawyer who had represented the Boston Strangler, Patty Hearst, the doctor in Chicago accused of murdering his wife whose case later became a movie, "The Fugitive," and who had been part of the "Dream Team" in the O.J. Simpson trial would be disbarred? Peter indicated that the hearing was being disputed and that there might be some cross-examination involved.

"I have no problem testifying as to what my own personal experience has been with Lee, and that I like him and respect his intellect (off the charts) but my experience is very limited," I told him.

He then handed me the transcript of the trial and the subsequent appeal of Lee's cases in Florida. Both transcripts were about three inches thick so I was starting to understand why Lee had asked me to testify. The hearing was in 10 days.

I testified at the hearing, answered a few questions presented by the opposing lawyer and I thought I was done. Other lawyers testified, both pro and con, and Lee also testified. I have always believed that there is a fine line between confidence and arrogance, and the penalty for crossing the line can be severe and take many forms.

Lee pushed the line a bit as many high-intellect people do, and he lost the argument for his licensing so he appealed to the state Supreme Court. I testified again, and again Lee lost. I was now five for five in the loss column! Lee went into the consulting business, wrote another book, and stayed in Maine.

Months later, Lee and I were scheduled to appear on Rob Baldacci's TV business show as business experts."

The first presenter on the show was trying to raise money to underwrite the development of a new vodka with the headquarters in Maine. After the presenter was done, each of the panel members were to opine on the business opportunity. I was one of the five so-called experts and I was scheduled to go last. When my turn came up, I said, "I feel I should disqualify myself as an expert because my background is in electronic engineering,

"I got Cs in chemistry and know nothing about the brewing business. The only thing I can say is I like vodka, have drunk far too much of it, and would suggest you talk to someone in the brewing business, and next time, bring samples!"

I was never asked back on the show.

Sailing makes for interesting friendships and attracts some interesting people. One of the fascinating men I've met in connection with the water was Mel Fisher.

I read a lot and especially books about the sea. I had picked up a book called "Treasure of the *Atocha*" some years earlier which was a story about a 16-year quest to find hidden treasure located in the remains *of Nuestra Senora de Atocha*, a Spanish galleon sunk in a hurricane in 1622.

I had met Mel when I visited his museum in Key West when I was also visiting the Hemingway house with the five toed cats. As I was exiting the museum, I stopped at the gift store on the way out and bought his book.

"Is Mr. Fisher in?" I asked the checkout clerk. "If he is, do you think he would autograph my book?"

"I'll see if he is here, give me your book, and just wait a minute." She came back a few minutes later and said, "Please follow me."

I still don't know why I was so lucky, but I was ushered into Mel Fisher's office.

"Why are you here?" he asked me.

"I'm a lover of the sea," I told him. "I served nine years in the US Navy, did some diving in the Navy, owned a lot of boats, and loved your story." I also expressed my condolences regarding his son and daughter-in-law. They died in a diving accident during his search.

He asked me a lot of questions. What I finally realized was that he was sizing me up as a possible investor. He still had a crew diving on the *Atocha* and he was selling shares in each year's quest. I finally realized his motives as he handed me some papers that outlined what a share in each year's venture could mean. Then I made an expensive mistake. I passed on investing $1,500 in his next search. They found $10 million!

FACING THE FAMILY

Heritage is like cash flow; it isn't important until you don't have any. Some people have very little interest in their heritage beyond their immediate parents and perhaps their grandparents and others pursue their beginnings as far as they can.

I had vowed privately not to pursue my heritage while my adoptive parents were still alive, out of respect for them and all they had done for me until they had passed away.

Then my mother left us in 1987. I received a phone call at night from the doctor in the nursing home where my mother was housed. She had developed severe Alzheimer's and no longer knew who anybody was, so my Dad and I had placed her there. He couldn't take care of her at home anymore.

I had never talked to this doctor before and as he introduced himself, I had the feeling that this was not going to be good.

It wasn't.

The doctor reported that my mother had fallen some time ago and had cut herself in the leg when she fell, and that the leg had become infected. He was calling me because a decision had to be made. He had called both my father and my sister and they had both said they couldn't do it, ask Dick."

"What's the decision?"

"The infection has spread and was now severe enough that to keep her alive, we will have to take her leg, or..."

"Or what?" I asked.

"Given the quality of life she will have without a leg, we can make sure she has no pain, but just let her go."

Wow! I thought. "How long do I have to make that decision?" I asked the doctor.

"I can't be exact, but probably 24 hours."

"I need to sleep on this," I told him. "I will call you tomorrow."

That was truly a life or death decision. I didn't sleep that night, I stayed up all night just thinking about it. Despite of all of our arguments and misunderstandings, I loved her.

This was really tough. I thought mostly about what kind of a woman she was. Her strength, her stubbornness, yet still able to share with me all the gifts she had given me. She very seldom showed emotions and while I never forgot her outburst when I showed her the adoption papers, she usually maintained her calm exterior. I tried to imagine what she would want to happen, for in a way, it was her decision. She had put up with all of my shit and still took care of me. I never lacked for a roof over my head, clean clothes, or a good square meal. She had had a full life, in her own way, a caring life. She was a proud woman and rightly so.

Like most people, I have often been faced with making decisions, some important, some minor. Those decisions were sometimes business related, sometimes family related, sometimes personal related. My decision-making process started evolving when I became a husband and a father. Before Andrea, David, and Laura, if I made the wrong personal decision I was the one that suffered. Now it was different.

In the professional world, particularly if you are in charge at any level, you don't own the workday hours. Your thinking time, reflective time, imaginative time, is at home, at night, on weekends. Those are the hours you own. The work hours belong to your employees. Those hours are spent solving the problems that they bring you.

Decisions are time-dependent so when confronted with a situation that required a decision, the first question I asked myself or the problem presenter was, “How much time do I have before a decision is required?”

The time equation is important because the right decision too late is no decision and may be even worse than the wrong decision. If you make the wrong decision at least you will get feedback so you can correct. No decision allows fate to deliver the outcome.

A smart man once said, “Knowledge without a voice is useless, a voice without knowledge is dangerous.”

More time is good, because it allows you to acquire knowledge, gather facts, talk to people, and do research, which generally results in a better decision. No time requires you to make a judgement call based upon your personal experiences, personal knowledge, your personal intuition. Unintended consequences, secondary and long-term impacts, often play second fiddle, and are not taken into account because of the lack of time.

A final screen that I have developed since the birth of my son, then my daughter, then my three grandchildren is a simple question:

“What would my children and grandchildren think of my decision? Would they be proud of me, or would they be disappointed in me?”

I never knowingly violated that edict.

That doesn't mean all my decisions have been the right ones! I have made some bad ones too! I have sold houses that I should not have sold, I have married people that I should not have married, and I have made some bad business decisions as well. You don't learn much from the right ones, but if you're paying attention you will learn a lot from the wrong ones.

Using that yardstick, I knew what I had to do. I called the doctor the next day.

"Let her go," I said.

"I understand," the doctor replied, "I think you are making the right decision." I didn't give a shit what he thought, this was about my mother. My sister and father never brought it up or ever talked about this decision. I have never forgotten her or this decision. Although I had two mothers, she was the one that took care of me and I regret to this day that I was not a better son.

She died two days later. It was 1987, she was 79 years old. I was 50.

Two years after my mother passed, the phone rang. It was Dad. Anytime a parent in their 80s calls you, the first question is, "Are you all right?"

"I'm fine, never felt better, but I just thought I would check in with you."

"That's great, Dad, I'm glad you called."

“Dick, I want you to know I’m thinking about getting married.”

“You what?”

“I’m thinking about getting married,” he said. “I’m lonely now, the house is empty, and I could use some help.”

“Dad, you’re 85 years old, and you want to get married?”

“Yes.”

“Do you have somebody in mind?”

“Yes, I do. It’s somebody I’ve known for a long time, she’s a retired nurse, a bit younger, but a good person.”

“Well, I guess that’s a good thing. Have you told my sister—your daughter—yet?”

“No, I haven’t called Marj yet, I was wondering if you...”

“Not on your life. That’s one call you’re going to have to make yourself!”

“Are you sure? I don’t know how she will react.”

‘Well Dad, that’s not a call I would want to make. You have my blessing if that helps.”

“Yeah, I guess I’ll have to.”

My sister who was very close to our mother, never forgave him.

Dad passed away in 1991. I had to pay for his funeral because the “bit younger” had taken everything.

* * *

I had never forgotten that moment in 1945 when I was eight years old and I had found my adoption papers and confronted my mother. I had never forgotten her anger or my confusion. The fact that I remember that incident some 63 years later speaks to the intensity that was my constant companion. The questions had stayed with me all those years, and in reality, had been a force driving me to prove that I was just as good as everybody else. There was also a level of suppressed anger because the truth had been kept from me. There was also anger surrounding the fact that I had been given away by my birth parents.

Why?

I had very little to go on; I had no birth certificate, no baptismal certificate, nothing, except the adoption notice changing my name. I still don't know if I was ever baptized. I still didn't know who my birth mother or father was. The laws of Michigan were very strict regarding the publication of adoption information as I was to find out.

I required a top security clearance in my work at MA/Com, which was very difficult to obtain (I had to take a lie detector test) because even the FBI could not penetrate the laws of Michigan. I had previously even hired a private detective agency who made an attempt then told me to forget it!

I knew from the adoption paper that my birth name was Gayle Eugene Llewelyn and that I was born in 1937. That was it.

Many false paths followed over the years. Sometimes when I ran into a brick wall, I was tempted to just quit. But somehow, I always shook it off and continued the search. When I was younger I would have crazy thoughts; I remember seeing my first homeless person on the street in Chicago when I was on weekend leave from Great Lakes and thinking that could be my father!

I sometimes felt like I was one of my boyhood heroes, John Wayne, in his hit movie, "The Searchers."

The search finally led me to a woman who was a Native American who worked in Michigan. Her primary objective was to locate Native American children and to convince them to rejoin the tribes, but she agreed to help me. We exchanged several letters and with her guidance, along with a new set of laws in Michigan that allowed the dissemination of certain classes of information that before had been protected and held secure, I was able to obtain information regarding my birth.

* * *

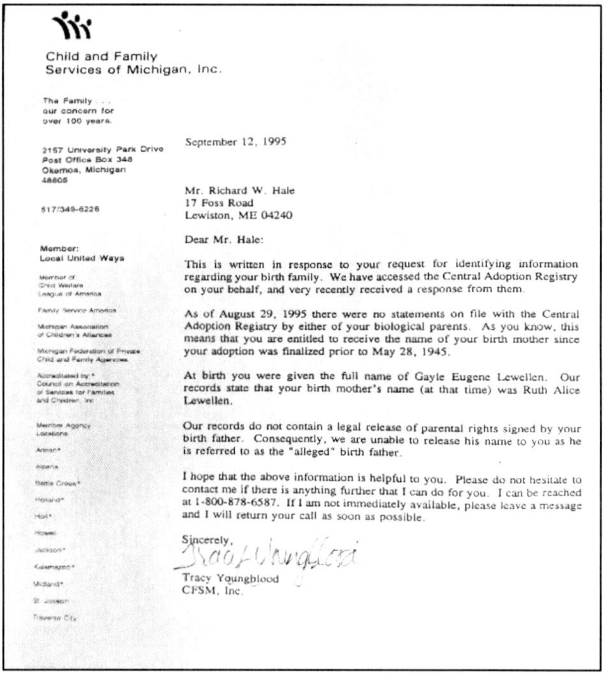

Child and Family
Services of Michigan, Inc.

The Family . . .
our concern for
over 100 years.

2157 University Park Drive
Post Office Box 348
Okemos, Michigan
48805

517/349-6226

Member:
Local United Ways

Member of
Child Welfare
League of America

Family Service America

Michigan Association
of Children's Alliances

Michigan Federation of Private
Child and Family Agencies

Accredited by *
Council on Accreditation
of Services for Families
and Children, Inc.

Member Agency
Locations

Adrian*

Alpena

Battle Creek*

Holland*

Holt*

Howell

Jackson*

Kalamazoo*

Midland*

St. Joseph

Traverse City

September 12, 1995

Mr. Richard W. Hale
17 Foss Road
Lewiston, ME 04240

Dear Mr. Hale:

This is written in response to your request for identifying information regarding your birth family. We have accessed the Central Adoption Registry on your behalf, and very recently received a response from them.

As of August 29, 1995 there were no statements on file with the Central Adoption Registry by either of your biological parents. As you know, this means that you are entitled to receive the name of your birth mother since your adoption was finalized prior to May 28, 1945.

At birth you were given the full name of Gayle Eugene Lewellen. Our records state that your birth mother's name (at that time) was Ruth Alice Lewellen.

Our records do not contain a legal release of parental rights signed by your birth father. Consequently, we are unable to release his name to you as he is referred to as the "alleged" birth father.

I hope that the above information is helpful to you. Please do not hesitate to contact me if there is anything further that I can do for you. I can be reached at 1-800-878-6587. If I am not immediately available, please leave a message and I will return your call as soon as possible.

Sincerely,

Tracy Youngblood
CFSM, Inc.

I stared at the envelope on my desk. knowing it contained a letter that probably denoted who my birth mother was. It was 1995. It was strange after all the bumps in the road to get to this point. I was almost scared to open the letter. After just staring at it for quite a while, thinking all the time about the long road traveled to get to this point, I said, "What the hell." and opened the letter.

The first contact with any family member was a phone call to Red, who lived in Muncie, Indiana. He was a musician who played string bass in a country western band. Red is a bit of a character, who is proud of the fact that he made his own wooden casket. He doesn't like phones, as evidenced by my attempts to make contact with him. I probably made at least 10 calls—and left messages—before he finally answered my call. It turned out Red was an uncle, my birth mother's brother. When I told Red the story and what I was attempting to do, his response was "I always wondered about Ruth's red hair!"

Red told me that I had a couple of brothers up in Michigan somewhere near Dewitt. This was a total surprise to me so I continued my search up into Michigan. I also told Red that I was planning a trip to Indiana to meet him. He never seemed to question my story, he just took it at face value.

This first contact was very exciting and the news that I had some brothers was really breathtaking. One of the problems, however, was that I now had to search for the name Kalso, as apparently my mother sometime after my birth had married a gentleman named Kalso.

My second contact was with a Michael Kalso who I thought might be a brother. As it turned out, the phone call was very disappointing.

Mike acknowledged who he was, and verified the names of Arch, Ruth Alice, and Llewelyn, as well as that he had a brother who lived in Dewitt named Russ. But he clearly did not want to talk about it any further.

Mike would not describe his father or verify that Ruth was buried in Lansing. He said that he did live in Haslett and that he did not have any kids.

I apologized for intruding.

Mike stated that he was not angry or mad at my contacting him, just that he did not want to be contacted in the future.

I decided that my next call had to be to Russ if I could find him!

Bingo!

Not wanting to make a mistake, I sat down and drafted a bunch of questions that needed to be answered and then tried to look at those questions from Russ's point of view. I worked the narrative over several times, trying to make it as non-threatening and yet as informative as possible.

Then I made the call.

Russ answered the phone and I identified myself and the purpose of the call.

"I'm calling in an effort to track down some possible relatives," I told him.

Russ was very skeptical and asked me several times, "What do you want?"

I explained that I lived in Maine, that I had several children and grandchildren and that I did not want anything. I explained my whole life background and that I had contacted Red and Mike in pursuit of the story. After some prodding from

Russ, I admitted that I thought we might have had the same mother. Russ said he had had enough but took my contact information and hung up.

About an hour later my phone rang, and Russ asked me if I was sitting down. I said I would.

"You have a brother!" he said.

Wow. My unmarried birth mother moved to Michigan from her home in Indiana when she became pregnant with me. She stayed with an aunt who was the only person alive who knew the story. Aunt Ethel had moved to Texas and was 92 years old. Russ called her and told her about my call. She broke down on the phone but verified the story. That prompted Russ's call back to me.

I told Russ that I had committed to meet Red in Muncie in about three weeks and would be staying in the local Holiday Inn. He said he and his wife were going to drive down from Michigan and meet me.

* * *

I stood outside the door knowing that on the other side of that one-inch-thick hollow-core plywood door, stood a brother that I had never seen! I had served in the US Navy for nine years all over the world, had played football, and been in many fights, had run a company with 8,000 employees,

First meeting: Brother Russ, Uncle Red, and me. December 2006

and had been searching for 21 years, yet I was scared to death!

"What the hell," I said and knocked on the door!

Russ and his wife Nita were on the other side of the door and had piled up many scrapbooks that I was to look at. Russ sat next to me and after turning many pages, Russ stopped.

"The next page will be a picture of our mother," he said. I slowly turned the page and started crying. I was 69 years old.

Red joined us later for dinner. Over the next 10 years. Russ and I have gone from being unknown to each other, to meeting, to being friends, to finally

Ruth, my birth mother

being brothers. He and Nita have been wonderful to me and I love them deeply.

I have no idea who my father was but I was able to track my mother's bloodline as far back as the 17th century, to Thomas Llewelyn Sr., 1620-1655.

His son, Morris Llewelyn, (1642-1730), contracted with William Penn, the founder of Pennsylvania, for 500 acres in America. Morris Llewelyn made the perilous three-month-long sail across the Atlantic Ocean with his wife and three children on the *Welcome*, one of Penn's fleet of colonization vessels, and arrived sometime in 1682 or early 1683. The trip was challenging; on some trans-Atlantic journeys a third of the passengers on died en route.

I mentioned a wife and three children. Morris had married Ann Young, (1647–1701), in 1673 in Wales. Morris settled in into the Haverford area of Pennsylvania north of what was to be known of as Philadelphia. Morris and his wife Ann Young built a first house of logs, and a year later started a stone house which still stands today. They were very active in the Friends Meeting House Quaker church in Haverford. In 1693, Morris is listed as a trustee. In 1698, Morris and his wife Ann, had a sixth child, a baby boy they named Samuel.

Samuel Edward Llewelyn became a wealthy planter in Wilmington Delaware. After the marriage of Samuel to the Widow Jones, the couple and her adopted son Jacob Jones migrated from Wilmington to Loudon County, Virginia where they lived until about 1770.

After moving to Virginia, they had a son named Thomas. The Llewelyns then moved across the Allegheny Mountains and settled on the Cheat River, establishing the Llewelyn Ferry.

In Monongalia County in what is now West Virginia, near the Pennsylvania line, Samuel Llewelyn obtained a grant of land in 1769. His name is prominently mentioned in the old records among the early settlers of the county. They helped found Forks of the Cheat Baptist Church, the first Baptist church in the region, at Stewartstown, West Virginia on November 5, 1775.

Samuel operated the first river ferry west of the Alleghenies. He and his wife were the key founders of the first Baptist church in the region Stewartstown, WV in 1774. The Forks of Cheat Church, named after the geography of the Cheat River area, is the oldest church in West Virginia west of the Allegheny Mountains.

Phillip Westley Llewelyn, 1794-1859

Samuel had eight children. The fifth child, a son named Thomas born in 1740, later fathered Philip Llewelyn, (1794–1859). Philip married Mary Ann Osborn. They in turn gave birth to two generations of men of God: Reverend Thomas Osborn Llewelyn and his son, Reverend Josephus Asbury Llewelyn, born January 20, 1848 in Randolph County Indiana.

Ann Osborn Llewelyn, 1800-1865

Josephus, a Methodist Episcopal minister in the North Indiana

Conference. He attended DePauw University, then known as Asbury University.

That leads us to my world. Rev. Josephus had a son named Arch Osborn Llewelyn, my grandfather. He was born in 1889 in Indiana and died there in 1975, just a state away from me. Arch, who became a Marine, married Valetta Atwood, my grandmother, in 1910. He never knew I existed because his daughter, Ruth, who was also my mother, gave me up at birth.

My newfound family began to fill in the blanks of my life; I marveled at how many traits we shared through the generations. I learned that my Grandfather Arch played the piano and when upset would sit down and play Beethoven's "Moonlight Sonata" to calm himself. I learned that my birth mother, Ruth, played the piano and organ; that my younger brother, Russ, plays bass guitar and has had his own band for many years. Even my Uncle Red, my mother's brother, plays upright bass in a band. It sure looks like my love of music was inherited.

As mentioned earlier, I play the piano and when my ship was back in San Diego, I got a job playing in a piano bar. I could play all of the old show tunes but always by ear as I could not read music. Many years later when I turned 80, I decided to take some lessons and see if I could learn how to read music which is a prerequisite to playing classical music. I am currently learning how to play "Moonlight Sonata."

Russ, my brother, has made it easier to come to grips with the family I never knew. He and his wife often visit me here in Florida, particularly during the winter because Michigan is not a place you want to be in January. We were shooting the bull as we always do, and Russ started to tell me about a story he had seen on TV, a *National Geographic* special. They watch a lot of TV in northern Michigan in the winter! I think it has something to do with the snow and cold. The episode was about Mel Fisher and his search for treasure. I pulled a book from my bookshelf and handed it to Russ.

"This has been autographed by Mel," I told him.

"Wow, you actually met him?"

"I did."

"Where?"

"In his office at the museum in Key West."

"Wow, can I borrow the book?"

"Yes, as long as you bring it back; I know where you live!"

In a way, Mel's 16-year search for treasure, and my 20-year search for my brother shared a lot of similarities. They had both taken a long time, they were both filled with success, sorrow, failure. Mel was looking for treasure and I was looking for my heritage. We were both in the end successful mainly through perseverance, stubbornness, and never giving up!

Anyway, Mel Fisher found his $400 million, and I found my family heritage. What are the chances that two long-lost brothers would be interested in the same story? For that matter, what are the chances that two brothers who didn't know that they even existed three years ago, would discover that they both loved music, that they both loved sailing and had sailboats?

Russ's boat was quite small, and when we both went out in it on eight-mile lake in northern Michigan, we almost swamped the damn thing. As it turned out, we both had an iceboat, and both loved cars. During Russ's trip I took him to the Muscle Car Museum here in Punta Gorda and he caught me staring at an old 1954 Cadillac Convertible.

"Why are you looking at that old Caddy?" Russ asked. He knew cars as he had worked for General Motors and retired from there after over 30 years.

"This is the same model car that I first got laid in!" I said.

Brother stuff.

The experience—not getting laid but getting to know my roots—has helped me renew bonds with members of my immediate family as well.

When Marjorie was about to be married, I was still in the Navy, but took some leave so that I could attend her wedding. When I got married recently at age 80, she came out from Arizona to attend my wedding.

Years later, Marj and her husband settled in Michigan with a home in Muskegon, overlooking Lake Michigan. We were to have many family reunions there with our kids and grandkids lounging on the beach having BBQs and playing games.

I remember one day we had everybody in stitches as she told about the time we were exploring stuff behind the garage and I provoked a hornet's nest. The hornets swarmed us and we both got at least 30 bites. We were both screaming as we ran into the house. Our mother made us lie down for the rest of the day as we fought off the poison in our systems.

At one of our family get-togethers at Marj's, we were divided up into cooking teams to ease the burden of feeding the herd. Because the reunions went on for two or three days, each team was responsible for putting on a lunch or dinner.

My team consisted of my son David and me. We were slated to go last. All of the previous teams tried to outdo the previous teams with wonderful meals. Then it became our time, for our last evening meal, and everybody anticipated a fabulous time.

David looked at me, I looked at him, and I said; "Is the teaspoon the big one or the small one?"

"I don't have the foggiest idea." David replied.

So we ordered pizza for everybody and had it delivered! My sister was not happy with another of her big brother's "fool ideas!" Great times, family times.

* * *

At my 80th birthday party, after everybody else was done telling lies about me, I was asked to say a few words. There were about 50 people in the room including my new-found brother and his wife, and my immediate family.

"I'm not sure exactly what I'm supposed to say, but I suppose that by the time you turn 80, you should have learned something, and be a little wiser and smarter," I said. "I'm not sure I am, but in looking back, I guess that I grew up an angry little boy and that anger worked in my favor because it drove me to prove that I was just as good as anybody else.

"I can only hope I have grown into someone who has learned at least a few things along the way and that some wisdom and judgement have rubbed off on me. About the only thing I am really sure about is that in the end it's not important how big your boat is, how big your house is, or how much money you have, what's really important is your relationship with your family and friends. The rest of it doesn't really matter."

LLEWELLYN THE LAST

In reviewing Welsh history I discovered that the Llewelyn name was revered in Wales. It has a legacy of kings, princes, and knights who fought battles with swords and longbows and laid siege to castles. So my search for my heritage led me across the water to Wales, a small nation located on the west central edge of England.

I was spurred to do so, perhaps, as one more means of connecting with my birth mother, who I learned had traveled to Wales to seek her heritage.

To try and get a head start on my journey I read seven books and countless articles about Wales and the Llewelyn story. We even rented a movie that some of you might remember "How Green is my Valley," which was one of the few movies ever made concerning Wales. By the way, the book that was the basis for the movie happened to have been written by Richard Llewelyn a Welshman. The movie won 5 Academy Awards in 1942.

To help facilitate our trip, I had contracted with a former professor of medieval history who had taught at the University of Wales and who now owned and operated a specialized tour group. As it turned out, in pursuing his doctorate, he had done his master's thesis on a member of the Llewelyn family. He turned out to be a wonderful guide, a

really nice guy who happened to have a special interest and knowledge in the Llewelyn story.

The country is very, very, pretty. It has mountains, rivers, waterfalls, beaches, forests, seaside inlets, and is very, very green. The country also has sheep everywhere!

The Welsh are famous for their singing and every village and town usually has a male choir. Once a year there is a nationwide contest between the choirs called an Eisteddfod. In high school I sang bass in the Acapella Choir and am happy to report that it was the only course where I got As. Where did my love of music come from?

I found the people to be very friendly and, above all else, very proud of being Welsh. During the ten days that I was there we visited 32 different sites that had significance as part of the Llewelyn saga. I

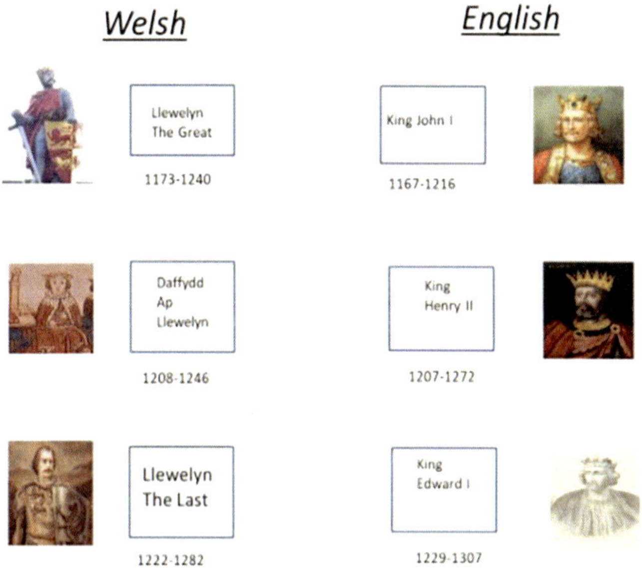

also spent an afternoon, at the National Library of Wales where I did a little bit of genealogy work.

While the Llewelyn saga covers over 400 years from 1000 AD to around 1410, I will concentrate on the three generations that were the focus of my trip. Their story is an epic of their lost struggle to maintain Welsh independence against the English, Scots and Irish.

Three generations of Llewelyns ruled Wales from around 1067 until 1283. Their antagonists were three generations of English kings who are also shown in the chart above.

Llewelyn the Great

On the top of the chart at the left, is Llewelyn Fawr, (Llewelyn the Great). He was born in 1172 in Dolwyddean Castle. Llewelyn the Great was both a warrior and a statesman and gradually became the ruler of all of Wales. In the process of accumulating his power, he became a perceived threat to King John of England.

In 1205, after a major battle between Llewelyn and the English, a treaty was signed, and King John gave his daughter, Joan, in marriage to Llewelyn to seal the pact.

After 25 years of marriage, Joan had an affair with William de Braose who got caught in Llewelyn's bedchambers. Llewelyn had de Braose hung in the marshlands below the ancestral home of Garth Celyn and Joan was placed under house arrest for a year. After a year, there was a reconciliation. Joan died in 1237.

One of the favorite Llewelyn stories told by the Welsh is about the king's favorite hunting dog, Gelert. Llewelyn returned from the day's hunting somewhat irritated as his dog had disappeared. When Llewelyn approached the lodge, he spotted the dog covered in blood. Worst of all, his newborn son was not to be seen. Llewelyn was enraged thinking the dog had killed his son. Llewelyn drew his sword and killed the dog. Moments later, one of

Lifting the elbow at the Llewelyn Pub

his knights found Llewelyn's son alive and unharmed. Lying next to him was a giant wolf that Gelert had slain in defense of the babe. Supposedly Llewelyn was so crestfallen by his mistake that he renamed the town in the dog's honor!

I visited this beautiful little town and had a beer in the "Llewelyn Pub." To maintain control over one's lands in those days, kings would constantly travel around the country where they stayed in their numerous castles, hunting lodges, or manors. One such area that I visited was on the island of Anglesey at a place called Aberffraw.

I stayed at Aberffraw on the grounds of the Court of Llewelyn at a building called Llys Llewelyn. In addition to his main house and several

St Beuno's Church, Aberffraw *By Phil Williams, CC BY-SA 2.0, https://commons.wikimedia.org/w/index.php?curid=9272057*

outbuildings that were used to house the people that accompanied him on these trips, he had built a beautiful chapel where he worshiped.

The chapel was called "The Chapel of the Princes." Services are still heard there. As it was a Sunday, I decided I would attend a service. When I walked into the church I was met by the female pastor who was very friendly and inquired as to who I was. I replied that I was an American and was investigating my Welsh ancestry and that my name was Llewelyn.

She was flabbergasted but welcomed me into the church which was named "Church of the Princes."

At the start of the service, she addressed the congregation and introduced me as "royalty from

On a trip to Wales, I was able to secure an appointment with the Gibson family who now own the property known as Aber Garth Celyn. Garth Celyn is located at the northern foot of the mountains of Snowdonia. It also looks out on the entrance to the Median strait, which separates the main body of Wales from the Welch island of Anglesey. The Gibsons had purchased the property thinking they were buying an old chicken farm only to discover they had purchased one of the homes of Llewelyn the Last. They discovered tunnels that ran from the basement up into the forest at the base of the mountains which was used as an escape path. The tower which I was allowed to go into was a lookout tower in the event the English were coming. I have to admit standing in the tower looking out the windows gave me a strange feeling to know that my ancestors had stood there some 700 years earlier.

Llewelyn coat of arms

America" and then conducted the service in both Welsh (the norm), and English in my honor.

I was both gratified and embarrassed. I am sure the congregation was upset because they had to sit through a double-long service!

While Llewelyn the Great had minor skirmishes over the next few years, 1234 marked the end of his military career, as the truce with King John and his successor, Henry III, held until Llewelyn's death in 1240. Llewelyn the Great had two sons, and three daughters. He chose his son Dafydd as his heir, which left the other son, Gruffydd, resentful. Gruffydd probably deserved to be a little miffed at life. After all, Dafydd was forced by Henry III to surrender Gruffydd as a hostage to guarantee the terms of the truce. Gruffydd was imprisoned by Henry III in the Tower of London. A few years later he fell to his death when his rope of bedsheets ripped as he was trying to escape the tower.

Llewelyn ap Gruffydd the son of Gruffydd, would go on to become Llewelyn the Last, Prince of Wales and, like his grandfather, ruler over all Wales. His younger brother Davydd was a very dramatic and charismatic young man with red hair like his father and would alternate between deep love for his brother and intense jealousy. He would betray Llewelyn the several times in the course of their relationship, and once actually plotted to kill him. Llewelyn's weakness was that he loved his brother, and while always exacting a price for his transgressions, ended up forgiving him. Davydd was always able to talk his way out of trouble, except in the end.

By this time, King Henry III had died, and was succeeded by his son, Edward I, the toughest of the three English kings that had tormented Wales and the Llewelyns.

King Edward I was very smart, ego-driven, tough, politically savvy, and devious. He was the destroyer of William Wallace as seen in the movie "Braveheart." Edward was constantly starting wars in order to gain more land and more power. As a result, he was extolling heavy taxes on the English so he was not very popular.

Llewelyn was tall, dark, loved to hunt, and was an excellent swordsman. He would have many battles with King Edward I, generally winning most of them. Although always outnumbered, the Welsh had their feared longbows and knew how to blend into the valleys and woods of their native land. Eventually, through weight of numbers, Llewelyn

The death of Llewelyn the Last

was forced into the mountains and agreed to negotiate a peace treaty.

King Edward sent the Archbishop of Canterbury to dictate terms, which called for Llewelyn to surrender all of his lands and power and subjugate his people to England. Llewelyn refused.

Six months later he was tricked into a meeting that was in fact an ambush. Llewelyn was killed fighting his way out of the trap,. His head was cut off, put on a stick, and carried to Edward as proof that Llewelyn the Last, Prince of Wales, was dead.

Thus the last Welsh Prince of Wales died fighting for freedom. To add insult to injury, Edward took Llewelyn's title and named his son Prince of Wales, a tradition that endures today.

His brother Davydd tried to continue the fight and avenge his brother, but was eventually captured, taken to London, and drawn and quartered. Don't Google that one—yuck!

As I stood at the tomb of Llewelyn the Last, I considered how my search for my mother had led me to this forsaken place. I looked out over the green land and thought of the years of waste as pride and anger led men to kill one another for pieces of land and bags of gold.

My own concerns, my own motives for travelling to the land of my ancestors seemed small and petty in comparison to wars that decided the fate of whole nations. But like those knights and lords of old, I had let anger and pride dictate too much of my life. In that place of battle where Llewelyn lost his crown and his life, I found a sense of peace. I felt I had come full circle. In finding out who I was, I discovered who I am.

At the tomb of Llewelyn the Last

* * *

A few months after my return from Wales I got a call from Lynne Lewellen Alber, a woman I had been working with on my ancestry. She was a distant relative who had caught the ancestry.com bug. Not necessarily a bad thing, but if you find yourself staring at the computer all day, day-dreaming about your relatives, or waking up in the night with cold sweats, you've got it! Lynne had it!

In one of our conversations I had mentioned my visit to Wales and that I had a lot of slides I could send her. Lynne lived in Indiana where a lot of my newly found relatives were living.

"Dick, would you consider coming out from Maine to Muncie if I were able to put together a group of our relatives to look at your slides and listen to you tell us about your trip?" she asked.

"Yes, I would be willing to do that," I replied.

A month later I flew out to Muncie and met Lynne. She showed me around town, then took me out to Mount Pleasant, a cemetery where a lot of my relatives were buried. Adjacent to the cemetery was a small church, where Josephus. my great-grandfather had preached.

COMPARISON

	MAINE	WALES
POPULATION	1,200,000	3,000,000
Sheep	560,000	15,000,000
SIZE		
N/S -	320 MILES	170 MILES
E/W -	190 MILES	60 MILES
Area -	30,862 m2	8,000m2

A chart from my Wales presentation

The next day, Lynn picked me up at my hotel and took me to a local restaurant where there were about 40 Llewelyns congregated—and all looking at me! Damn! As Lynne did the individual introductions, I was confronted with two Reds! My uncle, Ruth's brother, the first family contact I had made, had an absolute twin. Even more surprising, they had never met! You couldn't tell them apart! I'm sure there is probably an interesting story there, but I'm not touching it!

ENLIGHTENMENT

As I retired, one of the things on my bucket list was to write a book aimed at giving my children and grandchildren a vision as to their heritage. As I had never written a book, I started taking a class on writing at the local University here in Punta Gorda Florida where Diane and I settled in at our winter home. We have both given up on the Maine winters. After taking a class, I met James Abraham a book publisher of over 400 books, an editor, and writing coach. He has also become a friend and has helped me write my first book, an adventure book based on some of my personal experiences. The book is called "Never Give Up" and is primarily about some Navy Seals and PTSD.

Twenty veterans kill themselves every day in this great country. Why? Often, they destroy themselves because of some aspect of post-traumatic stress syndrome, or PTSD.

PTSD has been around for a long time, it's an old post-battle phenomenon with many names. It was 'Soldiers Heart' during the Civil War, 'Shell Shock' after WWI, 'Battle Fatigue' after WWII, 'Post Vietnam Syndrome' after Vietnam, and now 'PTSD,' post-traumatic stress disorder.

As long as there've been wars there've been victims. The wars may change but the causes have always been the same. They boil down to overwhelming guilt after having survived a lethal, horrific event.

A second major contributor, a feeling of low self-esteem when discharged into civilian life, is very common. If you were drafted or recruited out of high school, you probably have limited job skills. Those stresses can lead to depression, drug abuse, or excessive alcohol use and possible violent behavior. And even suicide.

In "Never Give Up," I address the problem of PTSD and offer what I hope are steps toward a solution. Some may say that there are existing services and institutions to take care of our vets, but consider this: back in April, three suicides occurred during a five-day period on Department of Veterans Affairs properties, supposedly where help is.

Suicide among veterans continues to be higher than the rest of the population, and younger veterans are particularly at risk. VA data released in 2019 showed the rate of suicide among veterans ages 18 to 34 had significantly increased.

In "Never Give Up," the lead character watches his friend survive 20 years of service only to kill himself because he could not adapt to civilian life. Now, before many in the audience scoff or suggest that PTSD is another modern namby-pamby fake disease, consider this: How many wives among you can talk about your nightmares, violent or depressed moods, or occasional inability to cope? How many have secret demons that manifest themselves in excessive drinking, irrational behavior, or feelings of guilt and remorse?

I'm a veteran and I know we have been taught to be men and keep our emotions locked inside. Well, you know what happens to a steam kettle without a vent.

I found a warm reception for my campaign to address PTSD during a speech in Punta Gorda.

Joe Carter, the hero of "Never Give Up," is a decorated Navy Seal who takes it upon himself to work with congressmen in drafting legislation to address the problem. The book outlines ways that we all can help reduce the tragedy of young men and women facing our enemies, then coming home to die by their own hands.

In the process of writing "Never Give Up" and doing the research, I came upon an idea that might be able to reduce the number of veteran suicides. The idea requires a new federal law, and I have had some discussions with and sitting Senators and congressmen about the same idea. However, the pandemic has taken all the air out of the room so nothing is happening currently. I am donating all proceeds from the book to the Wounded Warrior Project and the Navy Seal Foundation.

* * *

Not too long ago my wife and I downsized from a large home into a modest size condo. In the process of getting from point A to point B we decided to use a professional mover. The movers arrived at the house and started to load the furniture. I heard the older mover talking to the younger one about the service.

"I just got out of the Army after being stationed in Afghanistan," the young guy said.

The older mover asked if the young guy had seen combat. He responded that he had. At that point I mentioned that I was writing a book about the aftereffects of combat induced PTSD and wanted to ask the younger mover some questions.

As it turns out he was the typical modern-day soldier. He had been recruited right out of high school as he didn't have enough money to go on to college and had no skills so getting a job was tough. He went through basic training, learning how to handle a rifle, throw a grenade, fire a mortar, and duck. Next stop, rifleman, private, deployed to Afghanistan. Four deployments to the front, and he was out. He had no job, no skills except the aforementioned, and was now working as a mover's helper and felt like he had just wasted three years.

I asked him if he was still in contact with any of his Army buddies. He showed me a picture on his phone of three guys in battle dress. He said the guy in the middle had just committed suicide. He was married and had two kids. I thanked him for his service, remarked that I had served nine years and that I had lost a buddy as well which was why I was writing the book.

The mover finished the move, we shook hands, and I never saw him again.

* * *

Several months later, I received a phone call from a friend of 40 years. He is a Vietnam veteran who flew helicopters, saw combat, and in the process was exposed to Agent Orange. He has struggled at various levels of intensity over the years with both PTSD as well as health issues related to Agent Orange. In spite of his physical and emotional trauma, he has survived, has been happily married, and owns a small business with four employees here in Florida. He was 73 years old.

"I'm probably not thinking straight and need to talk to somebody I trust," he said.

He was overwhelmed by his personal situation. Because of the virus, his business revenue had gone to zero overnight, he was faced with laying off his four employees, and was probably going to have to file for bankruptcy. He told me that he didn't have enough money to keep going and he was concerned about his wife who he loved a lot. He had a life insurance policy for $250,000 that he thought would go to her if he died and he was considering suicide.

Many calls later, I thought he was back on the right track, with a plan, and committed to executing the plan, but still a long way from being out of the forest.

A week later I learned that he had a breakdown and was taken to the hospital, under restraints, where he was to await a bed in the psych ward. After a few days of waiting, he was admitted into the psych ward where he was supposedly treated and released two weeks later.

In talking to him, after he was released, he seemed like he was back on the road to recovery. I was a bit surprised by the fact that he had been released from the hospital, almost like he was being treated for a physical ailment instead of an emotional and mental issue which is generally much more complex and requires a different treatment timeline.

Ten days later he was dead.

He had hung himself in the garage of his home where his wife found him. He deeply loved his wife but had reached a place of despair so deep and dark that he had just given up.

I find myself both sad and angry. Sad at needlessly losing a long-term friend and angry at him for his selfish act. He abandoned his wife, family, and all of his friends of which he had many. He hurt me, one of his closest friends of 40 years.

His action called up some long-buried feelings of survivor's guilt which I thought I had under control. Could I have done more, why didn't I pay more attention, why didn't I make more of an effort? I failed him. If I could only have done more, would the outcome have been any different? I regret and am a bit angry about having to deal with all those questions again.

I believe that his latent service-related PTSD, and family issues all surfaced at the same time, capped off by the coronavirus dynamics that led him to the edge of the cliff.

PTSD, particularly if not treated, has a habit of lingering and then surfacing later in life. Of the 530 veterans committing suicide in Florida each year, and the 20 per day nationwide that commit suicide, a significant percentage are over 50 years of age, some over 70.

Death is forever and is one of the few absolutes in life. It can come in many forms, accidental, old age, or suicide. The first two we generally have very little to say about, but suicide is preventable which makes it even more tragic.

This experience reminds us how close some people are to that edge of the precipice. Despair, a feeling of hopelessness, loneliness, and fear, can lead us to actions that make no sense in the light of day, yet seemingly make sense in the darkness of the forest.

It's depressing to talk about depression. Why? Because depression if not combated, is so often the cause of even worst kinds of behavior. Everybody runs into depression some time in their life, the trick is to come up with a method, process, or way to climb out of the black hole into the light. Everybody has to find what works for them.

For me it is simple. I talk to myself; I say, "Hale, what the eff is wrong with you? You have it made; compare your life to those poor souls who have nothing or nobody to love or nobody that loves them. You've got it made, you are a lucky guy, quit bellyaching and feeling sorry for yourself, get off your ass, and do something!"

But it wasn't always like that. For example, I realize now that alcohol, my old friend, only made me forget that I was depressed. It didn't solve the problem, as a matter of fact it created new ones I had to deal with. Substance abuse is wrong, I know, but I also understand that sometimes it's all that keeps the demons from taking over.

* * *

There are two times when you are sure you know it all: first when you are a kid, then when you are an old fart. Wrong in both cases!

What I have discovered is that a writer is faced with many choices as to what kind of a book he or she is able or willing to write. A memoir, a biography, an autobiography, a historic novel, an action novel, a textbook, to name just a few.

I was recently asked by my editor and friend what kind of book was I writing, an action novel that doesn't require a lot of thinking, or a book that might cause the reader to think?

My reply was that it was a memoir that had two objectives; giving my kids and grandkids some sense of their heritage, and helping those that I love and care about avoid some of the black and blue marks that I had accumulated during my lifetime.

I didn't expect to sell any of these books, I just wanted to make available to my audience something that I never had and would have liked to have had.

What I discovered under this broad classification of "enlightenment" was that writing anything causes the writer to allow the reader a peek into the biases, prejudices, and beliefs, indeed the very character of the writer.

You cannot write for public consumption without exposing yourself at some level. I am coming to the belief that the type of book one is writing, can determine how much you allow the reader to see into your soul.

An action novel or soap opera type of book is read primarily for entertainment. Character development and complexity of plot can be tricky, but don't generally espouse life lessons. Its mission is to entertain, not to teach.

That's okay, I do it all the time. I started out reading books about submarines, and have read a lot of Tom Clancy's stories along the way. But as I was exposed to Thoreau's "Walden," some of Hemingway's stuff, Crane's "Red Badge of Courage," Dante's "Inferno," and many others, I started to learn that reading could also provide knowledge which was not only interesting and broadening, but also encouraged the creation of judgment and maturity.

I found writing this memoir more and more difficult as time went on because my editor (and still friend) kept challenging me to provide substance and even lessons learned with all of my experiences.

I have always been the guy who, upon walking into a crowded room, always stood in the back and quietly looked and listened. I never sought the spotlight in the center of the crowd. I sometimes found myself center stage but was never sure how I got there and it was never a place I coveted. I have always protected and guarded my innermost thoughts and feelings.

But now, in writing my memoir I find that I have to expose myself in order to reach my two goals. It is a scary process, this enlightenment stuff.

LOOSE MOOSE

I was, and still am, a proud member of a group of guys called "The Moose Group." The group was a bunch of guys that got their name due to the fact that they met in a bar/restaurant in Falmouth, Maine called "The Moose Crossing."

They met every Wednesday evening around 6 and sometimes lasted until closing. They did a lot of drinking, played Liar's Poker, told each other stories, talked about sports, politics, sailing, hunting, fishing, and women. I was introduced to the group when I first moved to Maine in 1987 by a real estate agent who was a senior member of the group and who became a good friend and a member of my sailing crew. His name was Frank (last names omitted to protect the semi-innocent).

I didn't make it every Wednesday but came close. These were good guys, and we enjoy each other's company. The group has morphed over the years and we have lost several of the members. I am probably now the oldest survivor.

One of the members lost was Frank. As we were sitting around one Wednesday evening, someone said, we should do something to honor him. As it turned out after talking about it, we decided to take up a collection and purchase a granite bench and see if the boatyard owner would allow us to place the bench on the small hill overlooking where Frank kept his boat. We all agreed that would be a perfect monument for Frank.

Scott, one of my closest friends as well as Frank's, and I were designated to find and purchase a granite bench.

Over the next several weeks we visited every funeral marker guy in southern Maine and tried to do a deal. The problem was we only had $500 which was about a third of the standard asking price. I knew that our chances of raising any more money from the Moose Group was pretty much nil.

Frank was a good guy but $500 was about the limit of his "goodness." While Scott and I were talking to the last monument guy, I noticed a picture on his wall of a lobster boat with a couple of guys pulling pots.

I asked the owner about the picture.

"That's a picture of me and my dad's boat."

I immediately started to talk about Frank's boat and what we were attempting to do for our buddy. The owner warmed up.

"I may have something for you, let's go take a look," he said.

He led us to a spot behind his shop where there was a bunch of snow-covered granite slabs that he described as mistakes. He pawed through several.

"I'll tell you what I'll do, I will build you a bench for five hundred dollars for your buddy Frank if Mr. Hale promises me he will take me and my wife out for a ride on his sailboat."

We agreed, but there was a catch.

"I'll have to turn the slab over because on the reverse side is the misspelled name "Mary Sue." I looked at Scott and he looked at me and I said, "You got a deal, when could we get it?"

"When are you putting your boat in the water?"

"Last week in May," I told him. It was March.

"I'll have it ready the last week in May. Give me your buddy's particulars—and can you get me a picture of his boat? I can engrave the picture on top of his bench along with his name."

"That would be outstanding."

We received the bench the last week in May and installed it at the site. Then we had another brilliant idea. At our next Moose Crossing meeting, someone said, "We should have a ceremony for Frank, invite his wife and family, and drink a toast to him."

"Great idea!"

Three weeks later, most of the Moose Group along with Frank's wife Judy, and their two older sons met at Frank's new bench, for a champagne toast. We were then going to the closest bar, "The Muddy Rudder," for a party in Frank's honor.

After I had taken the monument owner on a ride on *Bandito*, he gave us back the $500 so we had some money for the party.

"I sure hope Judy or his kids never look underneath the bench and see the mistake," I mentioned to Scott before the party.

"Don't worry about it, besides Frank is happy. He always said he would like to be on top of Mary Sue."

Scott and me with Frank's bench

At one of our planning meetings, as our get-togethers were always called, (we generally didn't plan anything) someone happened to mention that Valentine's Day was coming up and everybody was sure they were in trouble. Somehow, and I don't know how, I was elected to plan an event that would keep all of us out of trouble.

"It's going to cost you cheapskates some money!" I warned.

"That's okay," one wag said. "Just keep us out of trouble."

"Okay."

At the next week's meeting I outlined the plan.

“Here’s what we are going to do guys, I guarantee this will work! We will announce to each of your wives, girlfriends, or whatever, that they are going on a Valentine’s Day Mystery Trip and that they should dress up and be ready by 6 p.m.”

“I’ve chartered a large limo to go to each of the houses and pick them up. There will be champagne in the limo and each of them will receive a single rose. Then they will be driven around Portland, to confuse them, and then be brought to the restaurant where I have talked to the owner and we have reserved the upstairs private dining room.

“You guys don’t need to wear a tie, but you need to at least show up in a sport coat or suit. I’m probably in the most trouble, so I’m going to wear a suit, with a tie.

“The owner will, when the limo shows up, greet each of the ladies, and hand them another red rose as they are escorted up to the private dining room. At each place seating for the women, there will be another red rose, and a small box of candy. That’s where we will all be, waiting for them.

“After a great dinner and dessert, a barbershop quartet will sing love songs. That will be at 7:30.

“Guys, all of us will meet in the downstairs bar at 5 to have a drink, calm our nerves, and go over any last-minute details.”

There was a long silence.

Finally, Scott said, "How much is this going to cost?"

"I'm not sure yet, but I guarantee you'll all get laid after the event."

Appreciative silence.

The whole evening went on without a hitch!

One last note on the Moose Group. When Diane and I got married a couple of years ago, I invited all the key regulars thinking they wouldn't show up since the wedding was in Florida.

They showed up!

LOVE AND MARRIAGES

I guess I wouldn't have to have a separate category for my wives if there hadn't been so many of them!

My first wife was Andrea Maniglia, to whom I was married from 1961 to 1979. She is the mother of my children and grandmother to my three grandchildren. Our marriage lasted 18 years and produced two wonderful children and three beautiful grandchildren.

When Addington Laboratories was sold and I accepted the job with Omni Spectra, we had to move to New Hampshire. Andrea and I were having some problems in the marriage but I think we both thought a move might help. Two houses and several years later, we both decided the marriage wasn't working out so we called it quits. I continued to see both David and Laura and we spent a lot of time racing sailboats together until they both went on to college.

Linda Decker, to whom I was married from 1982 to 1992, was a very attractive waitress at a local high-end restaurant in Merrimack, New Hampshire, where I frequently had held quarterly business meetings. I also visited the restaurant in between the meetings and after some time started dating Linda. She had two young children, Todd and Adam and she was struggling as a single mom. After several months of dating she proposed to me, and while a bit uncertain, I said yes. It was a mistake. I should have said no.

Ten years later I asked for and received what turned out to be a very expensive divorce. There is an old saying, if you can't say anything good, keep your mouth shut! Enough said.

Janice Peterson was my wife from 2003 to 2012 Having had bad experiences with marriage, I was certainly not interested in jumping back into another one! I dated a bit with Janice, a woman I had known for several years. Janice was a single mom with two grown daughters, both who were through college.

Her brother was a minister and she came from a strong family in Minnesota. She was of Swedish and Norwegian descent, quiet, and always a bit reserved. In my years as a single man between Linda and Janice, I had done a lot of sailing, and hung out with the sailing crowd that were a bit rowdy from time to time. I also had a group of guys that were my drinking buddies as we got together once a week and told lies to each other. This was my world. I was also a member of the Portland Yacht Club. I was probably drinking too much, a habit hard to break that would come back to haunt me later. At any rate, after several years of off and on dating, I proposed marriage, she accepted, and we got married.

She moved into my bachelor house which I had dubbed Dick's Last Resort with one proviso —that I would sell the house and agree to buy a new place that we would start together within one year after the marriage. I agreed.

About a month before she moved in, she called me and asked me if it would be okay if she burned some incense in the house.

"What for?"

"It will just provide a cleansing aroma and take out any bad effects in the house."

I said, "No problem, do what you have to do." As I thought about it as I was driving to work, I called her back.

"How big a fire are we talking about?" I had to ask.

Anyway, it was a good marriage. She had many friends in and around Freeport, Maine close to Falmouth, Maine where I had settled after the Linda divorce and our social life started to revolve around her world at the expense of my friendships and relationships. After almost ten years, I was no longer a member of the Portland Yacht Club as I had sold my 47-foot racing sailboat. She didn't like racing or all the partying that came with it—or some of the people.

I didn't own my waterfront house next to the yacht club where I could also look out at my moored boat I was not racing anymore, had no boat and had pretty well given up my drinking buddies and our Wednesday night get-togethers. My life had changed. All of the things that were important to me were gone.

Janice was and remains a good person and after seeing a counselor for about a year, it was with great reluctance that I came to the conclusion that I should move on. So I asked for and received yet another divorce. There was several other life dynamics militating against me that I am still working through. Janice is a good person, and probably deserved better.

I was single for a while until one day Scott, a Moose Crossing friend, gave me a call.

"Hey Dick, I've got this friend that I work with, she's single, full of energy, and I think you guys would get along great. What do you think?"

Diane Leblanc's photo changed my life.

"Tell me about the energy bit, how much are we talking about? You know I'm in my late 70s and not dating."

"A lot."

"Got any pictures?"

"I'll send you a couple."

A day later the phone rang, it was Scott again.

"What do you think?"

"Looks like a handful!" Little did I know.

"So, what's the verdict?"

"This is a blind date, so how about if we double date with you and your girlfriend," I said, "just in case?"

"OK, I'll send you her address and tell her you'll pick her up at 6 Saturday."

So on August 17, 2013, I drove up to Diane's house. I had my tan slacks, and blue blazer on and as I walked up the front stairs there on the porch she sat. We exchanged greetings and I walked her to the car. Holding her door open as I always do, I waited until she was seated before closing the door. Thank my mother for good manners—later Diane told me how much that impressed her. We drove to the Saltwater Grill and enjoyed a quiet dinner because

Scott and his girlfriend were not speaking. She was mad at Scott.

Diane and I got along very well. She had married her high school sweetheart, had two grown children and now had three grandchildren. She had been married for 30 years and single for quite a while. I skipped over my matrimonial background and kept the conversation on other subjects. Then she rested her hand on my leg at the dinner table and that, as they say, was that. We never looked back. Diane and I dated for the next five years and were married on November 17, 2018. She has been the light of my life, and I look forward to spending the rest of my life with her.

Diane has been great and has taught me what love is really about. She lights up a room when she enters and her positive attitude and enthusiasm capture your heart. Diane makes me to want to be a better man.

It is clear that there are a lot more adventures to be written about Diane and my story, and I look forward to living long enough to write about them!

Keith, Wendy, Steve, Stacy, Diane, Dick,